ROSS GARNER

mission-shaped
parish

traditional church in a changing context

Paul Bayes and Tim Sledge

with John Holbrook, Mark Rylands and Martin Seeley

CHURCH HOUSE
PUBLISHING

Church House Publishing
Church House
Great Smith Street
London SW1P 3NZ

ISBN 978-0-7151-4204-2

Published 2006 by Church House Publishing

Second impression 2009

Printed by MPG Books Ltd
Bodmin, Cornwall

Contents

Series introduction

In adopting and commending the *Mission-shaped Church* report, the Church of England took an important step forward in its understanding of God's mission. It is a journey full of opportunities and challenges, and one which opens up new questions. This series of titles is designed to resource thinking, reflection and action as the journey continues.

Each title in the *Mission-shaped* series considers how the principles presented in *Mission-shaped Church* can be applied in different areas of the Church's life and mission – in work with children and young people, in rural areas, in traditional parish church life and in the area of apostolic spirituality. What perspectives, and inner values are necessary to be part of a mission-shaped Church today? These areas were touched upon in the MSC report but are now explored in more depth.

All the authors write with the benefit of years of practical experience. The real-life case studies and practical examples they provide are designed both to be inspirational models of ministry and mission and to be adapted by the reader for their own context.

The examples cited include both 'fresh expressions', developed as a response to the culture of a particular group of people, and more traditional models, reflecting the fact that 'there are many ways in which the reality of "church" can exist'.[1] This series is firmly committed to advocating a mixed economy model for the Church of the future.

---

[1] Archbishop Rowan Williams, from the Foreword to *Mission-shaped Church*, GS 1523, Church House Publishing, 2004.

Acknowledgements

This book is rooted in God's gracious activity among people in the places where we have been called to serve. We are full of thanksgiving in being part of their lives and the lives of the communities for various periods of time. To all of them we want to say thank you.

Particularly, Paul thanks the Christian communities at St Paul's Whitley Bay; the West London University Chaplaincy; St John's, Desborough Road and the High Wycombe Team Ministry; St Winfrid's, Testwood and the Totton Team Ministry; and all their countless small groups and cell groups. Thanks too to friends and colleagues in ministry in all those places and networks, especially Kate, Peter, David, Jillian, Carol, Ruth, Beren, Maureen, Derek, Tony, Lyn and Emma.

Tim would like to thank the Christian communities of the Peterborough Diocese and of St Mary's, Luddenden with Luddendenfoot, St Peter's, Sowerby and St Mary's, Cottonstones near Halifax. Thank you also to my colleagues on Leading Your Church into Growth course, particularly John Holmes, Robin Gamble, John Young, Ann Hemsworth – four Canons with attitude, fun and deep wisdom who taught me that this process is all about a desire to see lives and communities changed through an encounter with Jesus Christ.

We would both like to thank our editor Kathryn Pritchard whose heady cocktail of comment, exhortation and encouragement has kept us on task through this project.

Paul Bayes and Tim Sledge   Feast of St Francis of Assisi 2006

Foreword

I sometimes hear grumbles that excessive attention is being given to 'fresh expressions' in the wake of the *Mission-shaped Church* report. Critics argue that the opportunities offered by old ways of being church are being neglected. At the same time it is hard to pretend that all our established parishes live by the truth that God's mission is the business of the Church.

This contribution to the 'Mission-shaped' series is both full of confidence about the missionary potential of traditional parish church ministry and has some helpful reflections on how aspirations can be turned into greater reality. Written by experienced practitioners every page of this book describes a Church of England with which I am familiar. I imagine that most readers will smile ruefully at the definition given of the deanery synod as 'a group of Anglicans waiting to go home'. These are no ivory tower reflections but suggestions from a group of dedicated ministers who have tried out their advice and found that it works.

I can imagine parish groups finding it useful to take each chapter in turn and prayerfully over the period of a year to stimulate thought and action about what needs to change if God's mission is to be in truth the business of the Church. That does not, of course, mean that every word in these pages is to be taken as gospel. I found myself disagreeing violently at several points and wanting to argue back, but that is also part of what makes this book useful.

We all need this kind of self-examination. I have never, in more than a decade of being a bishop, visited a church where parishioners were not prepared to say something like 'we are a very welcoming church'. Yet more than a few churches in my experience are virtually un-joinable and are even so lacking in awareness that they blame this state of affairs on those who come once and never again. The parish church that is genuinely open to God's mission and accessible to its community, and where people with unlike life stories can encounter one another as friends in our highly compartmentalized society, is an ancient idea that is always fresh.

I pray that the reflections in this book may advance the cause of that 'mixed economy' in the Church of which our Archbishop has spoken.

Richard Chartres
Bishop of London

Feast of St Vincent de Paul

Preface

Paul Bayes

If books on mission are criticized it's usually for what they leave out. So here, at the beginning of our book, I want to tell you what's in the tin – and what we've had to leave out.

- This book is about the *Church*, although of course the whole mission of God in the world is far greater than the Church.

- This book is about some of the Church's *practices*, although of course the mission of God through the Church is far greater than what Christians do when they meet together. It's not about 'mission initiatives' in churches. It's about the bread-and-butter things that churches do, seen through the lens of mission.

- This book is about some of the Church's *traditional* practices, although of course the mission of God in the Church's practices is far greater than the traditional, and crucially includes among other things fresh expressions of church and church planting.

- This book is about some of the Church's traditional practices *in a changing context* – and here perhaps all can agree that things are changing, changing faster than anyone can fully grasp.

Five people have contributed to this book, all of us clergy. Between us we have been ordained for over a hundred years. Most of our lives have not been spent as professional experts or theologians. We have whatever expertise and theology comes from trying to make parish churches work as centres of mission and love in this changing context.

Since 2004 the Church has been inspired and helped in its work by *Mission-shaped Church*, the best-selling General Synod report that leads the Church to explore 'church planting and fresh expressions of church in a changing context'. Encouraged by its warm welcome in the churches, a whole range of new initiatives are springing up all over the country.

Every local church should be asking whether a fresh expression should be part of its mission. Already hundreds of fresh expressions of church are telling their stories and sharing their experience and enthusiasm – for example through the website of the joint initiative of the Archbishops of Canterbury and York and the Methodist Church, 'Fresh Expressions' (www.freshexpressions.org.uk). All this is terrific and we want to be part of it.

But alongside this we are also committed to the parish church and its traditional practices as a vehicle for the mission of God. In other words we believe in a 'mixed-economy Church'. This phrase is Archbishop Rowan Williams'. In his first presidential address to the General Synod, in 2003, eight months before *Mission-shaped Church* was published, he said this:

> Tearing up the rule book and trying to replace the parochial system is a recipe for disaster and wasted energy. In all kinds of places, the parochial system is working remarkably. It's just that we are increasingly aware of the contexts where it simply isn't capable of making an impact, where something has to grow out of it or alongside it, not as a rival (why do we cast so much of our Christian life in terms of competition?) but as an attempt to answer questions that the parish system was never meant to answer.[1]

'In all kinds of places, the parochial system is working remarkably.' We've written *Mission-shaped Parish* to unpack a few of the lessons that might be drawn from that. We want to remember that parish churches can act both as springboards for the new, and as vessels of God's mission in their own right. And we want to draw out some of the lessons of *Mission-shaped Church* – especially in its talk of mission values – for parish clergy and leaders.

Unchurched, dechurched

> I hanker after clarity in the wider Church about the different courses that can be broadly set, depending on where we need to travel to.[2]

There are essentially two mission fields, white for harvest, in the UK today. They overlap and blur, because nothing is simple when it comes to people. Yet they call for distinct responses from the Church in this generation.

The largest, growing group is the 'unchurched', those whom the Church has never reached or touched.[3] For them the world of Christendom is past and gone. They are not thereby cut off from spirituality, or from the call of God. But the voice of the Church itself sounds no echo in their hearts. A fresh expression of church can mediate the Good News of Jesus Christ to them in a way that makes sense of their own longings and their lives. The Church rightly needs to put enormous energy and resources into listening, responding and being with them. Mere tokenism – for example, a single nightclub church in every diocese – is not enough. Increasingly the unchurched are the future, and increasingly the Church of the future must make them its priority. We take all this as read.

But then there is the group called the 'open dechurched'. These are people who still live in the shadow of Christendom. They have been in close touch with the Christian community but have now drifted away, although they are open (and will often say they are 'likely') to return. In many ways this group is the most baffling of all. Researchers find it hard to agree on how large it is. Some polls report that it comprises less than 20 per cent of the population, others well over 40 per cent. This is because the people in it give widely differing answers to quite similar questions about their religious lives. Their spirituality is a mystery both to them and to us. They are not on the fringe of the Church, but they are not a million miles away either. For them the inherited richness of the Church is potentially reachable and helpful, so long as it is mediated with humanity and a light touch. For them a mission-shaped parish church can be a vehicle of salvation, of the mission of God.

Values first

This book moves through three stages. First, when a parish church shapes up for mission, the process begins by being clear about values. The values of a local church will flow from God's call and purpose, and will make it much easier and clearer to ask what that means locally in terms of the church's strategy and activities. So we look at the five values that *Mission-shaped Church* sees as vital. Secondly, in a number of brief 'snapshots' we go on to look at how those values have been worked out in the history of the Church in England. And thirdly, in the main part of the book, we focus on some of the things any parish church does day by day: its worship, its pastoral contacts with people at critical points in their lives, its relationship to the civic and public structures of its community, the way it nurtures and develops faith in its new believers, its administration and government – all this seen from the point of view of the mission of God.

Three authors bring specialist contributions to this book. In Chapter 5 Martin Seeley reflects on life and ministry in an urban setting and the surprising results of listening to the local community. In Chapter 7, John Holbrook, Rector of Wimborne Minster in the Diocese of Salisbury, reflects on the life and ministry of the civic church in the light of mission. Today's cathedrals function, to all intents and purposes, as parish churches for many in their localities. For this reason we have included a chapter (10) in which Mark Rylands reflects on cathedral ministry in the light of the mission values of *Mission-shaped Church*.

One of our fundamental points is that there are no quick answers. Indeed the point is not to be looking for those, but to be asking the right questions. *Mission-shaped Church* is full of stories and examples of good practice; but simply pinching a few of these for your own church is absolutely not recommended.

We're trying to build on a tradition of mission thinking which sees the mission of God as the mother, or at least the midwife, of the Church: 'It's not the church of God that has a mission in the world, but the God of mission who has a church in the world.'⁴ To use another image, God's mission is the chisel that shapes the Church – God's mission, not the cultural preferences, nor the comfort, of the Christians themselves.

This can be a hard saying. Any expression of church can be shaped for mission, provided it takes its shape and its heart from what God has revealed and what the culture is saying. This is as true of BCP matins as it is of alt.worship. All the same, Christian believers whose entire life has been built around certain liturgies, systems and orders will not find it easy to disentangle their own preferences from the call of God to be faithful. The very gospel that they have received over the years, that has purified and strengthened their hearts as disciples, runs the risk of becoming a consumer choice and a comfort-blanket that smothers the mission of God. It's at that point that those years of exposure to the good news of God's love, those years of conformity to the pattern of Jesus, receive their acid test.

But we know that all through the life of the Church in England the mission values have indeed produced, informed and invested change and renewal. Time and again the parish churches of England have acted generously, lived out their faith, and built their lives on a mission foundation. Much that is now held dear as safely traditional was, when it began, a daring mission initiative.

Every day church councils and clergy are still making hard choices, using the good things that they have inherited for God's mission. Our book tries to point to the spiritual realities that underlie all this, and to sketch what these things might mean in the bread-and-butter work of all parish churches. You have read this far, so you are already on board. We hope and pray that you will enjoy the ride!

The value of values

Paul Bayes

Build mission-centred values at the heart of the church as it is.[1]

We do what we value and we value what we do.[2]

Tie-break!

 In St Mungo's PCC it is time for the treasurer's report as usual. Shoulders slump around the room, in anticipation. But astonishingly the treasurer is smiling; she has received some good news and has been saving it until now to surprise everyone. Mrs Johnson, a long-standing member of the church who died peacefully a few months ago, has left St Mungo's the residue of her estate and it is a six-figure sum. Best of all – the bequest comes with no strings attached!

A delighted hubbub breaks out and then the ideas begin to flow. Pay the parish share? No, pay off our debt! Redecorate the church? No, a new carpet! A new sound system for the worship group? No, renovate the organ! A disabled toilet? No, a new kitchen! A new administrator? No, a new youth worker! Give ten per cent to Tearfund? No, to Christian Aid!

A loud voice rises above the rest. Mrs Johnson was on the flower arranging team – why not give them two hundred pounds a week for ten years to make the church look really glorious? And we could have a lovely new set of vases in her memory, each with a brass plaque! Others feel that this might not be quite right – but how do you say so without seeming to belittle Mrs Johnson?

The hubbub increases but somehow the delight seems to be vanishing. Almost every one of the ideas seems good and most of them seem necessary and even urgent. But the trouble is that, even with what the PCC is now calling the Johnson Fund, there are simply not enough resources to go around.

From the chair the vicar tries to get a grip, but he's not sure what to say. He watches the ideas fly around the room with a sinking pastoral heart. The curate is being icily polite with Mr Alderson over whether the choir needs new robes. The curate thinks not – 'with all due respect'. The vicar knows what that means, and he hopes they won't come to blows before coffee.

Then a possible solution – the PCC's resident diplomat is talking enthusiastically – why not just split the bequest and support everything? But now the treasurer is looking gloomy as the huge bequest shrinks before her eyes into 20 or more small projects, each of which will need matched funding from somewhere. In the Council a grumble begins to gather strength – why, oh why, didn't Mrs Johnson just tell us what to do with her money? And the treasurer wishes she had never mentioned the bequest – or at least that she'd bought a crash helmet first . . .

This scene is both unfamiliar and all too familiar. Unfamiliar because generous bequests from parishioners, although not unheard of, are not *that* common. All too familiar because at every level of church life the topics that are debated are like icebergs, floating on a sea of assumptions and values, 90 per cent of which are not in view. So for those who are trying to build mission-shaped parish life, a vital part of the task must be opening these values to inspection.

This isn't easy. Parish life is hectic, and urgent matters crowd in all the time. Most churches find it very hard to give people space to reflect together on the reasons why decisions are made, and on exactly why their leaders make the choices they do.

The problem at St Mungo's is quite specific. Between the preaching of God's word in worship on the one hand, and the decisions of the church council on the other, there is a missing link. Despite his pastoral heart, their vicar has not equipped St Mungo's PCC for their work. They are trying to build their church on decisions without foundations. And yet it could have been so different. Long before that meeting, a shared and owned *vision* of God's *purposes* and a set of shared values could have issued in a *strategy*.

More management-speak? Or something more Godly? Bishop John Taylor, writing in the 1970s in his wonderful, prophetic book *Enough is Enough*, points to an answer: Perhaps we might learn, he says:

> by taking as our model, for example, the suburban parish
> which was looking forward to its centenary gift-day as a
> chance to redecorate the rather shabby interior of its church
> and refurnish its sanctuary. Then came Bangladesh: and that
> church remains shabby, and more truly glorious.[3]

Unlike our fictional St Mungo's, the suburban parish in this real-life story did not have the money in the bank. Like most churches they had a plan, and they were aiming to do some good things but not others. Renovating the church, helping the poor – maybe there was no clear winner, maybe it was a tie. But they had to choose, to break the tie. And, again unlike St Mungo's, it seems they had a clear, agreed vision of God's call on them, and some values. All this gave them a tool, a tie-breaker, so that when they had to choose between good things, they could say 'yes' to some and 'no' or 'not yet' to others.

Strategy with a human face

There doesn't have to be anything mechanistic or driven about this process. It is true that talk of 'strategy' can be annoying, and indeed it can bring out the worst in the people who defend it as well as those who dislike it. Jesus seems to have managed pretty well without using it. All the same, despite its military–industrial flavour, the word points to a good and necessary process for any local church. We believe that strategic planning is one of the many tools that are necessary for the local church to flourish. What prevents 'strategy' from becoming hard-edged and unlovely is ensuring that it is built on a Christian foundation – and that means a foundation of values based on faith. Values are the hinge. They swing what we know of God into action, and bring the theology of a church to bear on its practice.

The dynamic can be seen like this:

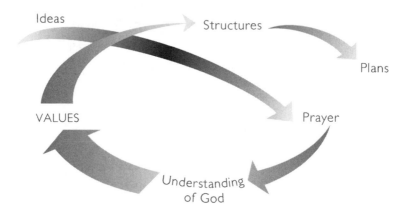

Ideas → Structures → Plans → Prayer → Understanding of God → VALUES

Every person and every institution has values – and usually it is the unexamined ones that are held most dear. In laying their mission foundation a local church doesn't have to ignore anyone's values, but it will have to put them in a particular order for the time being.

Back at St Mungo's Mr Alderson's values include offering good and well-ordered worship to God. The curate would not disagree with this, but perhaps she values relevance in mission even more highly. So they argue with each other – but when they almost come to blows, both of them think it is not over values but over robes.

And what was happening with the other PCC, the real-life suburban parish in the case study earlier? Perhaps it was this – that the Bangladeshi famine spoke to their understanding of God as one who loves the poor. And because they were a church that highly valued helping the poor, the hinge to action swung smoothly and cleanly and their finance committee knew what to do. Not without argument and debate, no doubt – they too may have had their Mr Aldersons – but in the end this common concern to help the poor was the basis for a corporate vision and an agreed strategy, although perhaps they would not have put it that way. Perhaps they would have said they were just doing the obvious thing, the right thing.

So every church has values, whether explicit or not; and almost every church thinks it's doing the right thing. But if a church has *mission-centred* values then its understanding of God is of one who is love, and who sends love.

Like the rest of the worldwide Christian family, the authors of *Mission-shaped Church* are deeply indebted to the great South African missiologist David Bosch, whose 1991 book *Transforming Mission* is such a gift and resource to the Church, and whose early death in a car crash was such a loss. In his book Bosch writes: 'Mission has its origin in the heart of God. God is a fountain of sending love. This is the deepest source of mission. It is impossible to penetrate deeper still: *there is mission because God loves people.*'[4]

If that's your understanding of God then your values will move you to mission. This will not be because mission is the flavour of the month, or *Mission-shaped Church* the book of the last few years. It will not even be because the bishop tells us there's a need to get something done. It will be because God is who God is.

> In the new image mission is not primarily an activity of the church, but an attribute of God.
>
> (David Bosch)[5]

Mission-shaped Church follows this way, and its life and theology are rooted here. In the middle of the report there is a list of fresh expressions of church, each with its stories and its reasons. Then follows the theological centre of the book, reflecting on all this good practice. But in the hinge-place, between the stories and the theology, there come the report's five values:

Mission-shaped values

> [The missionary values] are intended to offer a framework that can be applied to an existing local church or to any strategy to develop, grow or plant a church or a fresh expression of church ... (they) provide a broad standard to

help discernment at a time when the shape of the Church of England is increasingly varied and in flux.[6]

- **A missionary church is focused on God the Trinity**

Worship lies at the heart of a missionary church, and to love and know God as Father, Son and Spirit is its chief inspiration and primary purpose . . .

- **A missionary church is incarnational**

It seeks to shape itself in relation to the culture in which it is located or to which it is called . . .

- **A missionary church is transformational**

It exists for the transformation of the community that it serves, through the power of the Gospel and the Holy Spirit . . .

- **A missionary church makes disciples**

It is active in calling people to faith in Jesus Christ . . . It encourages the gifting and vocation of all the people of God, and invests in the development of leaders. It is concerned for the transformation of individuals, as well as for the transformation of communities.

- **A missionary church is relational**

. . . It is characterized by welcome and hospitality. Its ethos and style are open to change when new members join.[7]

The trouble with lists of values is that if they stand alone, they're just a collection of abstract nouns. But clarifying values, making them concrete – really working at what they will mean locally – is the best practical first step any local church can take in its mission planning. This is because, in a church like ours, clear values are the sovereign remedy for anxiety.

Mission values and anxiety

'Hrum, Hoom', murmured the voice, a very deep voice like a very deep woodwind instrument. 'Very odd indeed! Do not be hasty, that is my motto.'

(Treebeard the Ent, in J. R. R. Tolkien, *The Two Towers*)

In the West the twenty-first century-Church is living through anxious and fretful times. Christian believers look around and see evidence of churches in numerical decline. Often the Church in general, and in England the Anglican Church in particular, sees all that it holds dear in faith questioned and, as likely as not, ridiculed. So nervousness, and a twitchy desire to find the quick fix, become endemic.

This isn't helped by our context. In the West Christians live in a society where the ability to get on and get things done is highly prized and, ever since the 1960s, secular thinking has used the word 'theology' to mean pointless and useless nattering.

All this makes for a church that would not please Treebeard. Many of us have become extremely hasty. Badly wanting to get on with God's work, and feeling the urgency acutely, church people are tempted to move into action straight away. It's such a temptation to grab the latest ideas from somewhere else and try to put them into practice, without thinking for too long about why they were crafted and shaped in their particular way for their particular context.

This anxious grasping holds as true for pastoral care, liturgy and the ordering of buildings as it does for mission – but mission and evangelism are peculiarly prone to it. It's fatally easy for churches to see mission and evangelism as practical, down-to-earth, active 'things' for Christians to do – to do, that is, if they like those sorts of things.

There is no doubt that seeing mission in this fragmented way has 'advantages' for the whole Church. It produces two kinds of quiet life. On the one hand it has left a field clear for passionate and active 'mission-minded' people to generate a thousand ideas before lunch and see them die unmourned by supper time. And on the other, it has given freedom and space to the rest of the Church to let the activists get on with it – with a sigh of relief.

This is an exaggeration. But if you look around your church, deanery or district you may find places where it isn't too far from the truth. In those places, despite the inspirational theology of David Bosch and many others, 'mission' has become a fringe activity and even an optional extra – with a handful of new initiatives every year, rather a frantic flavour, and very little continuity or ownership. When this happens in a local church the mission of God can get lost, either in anxious activism or in endless talk.

More than anything else it has been the intention of *Mission-shaped Church* to change this mindset. Churches that take the report seriously know that it asks them to stop and look around – at their context and their potential, yes; but before that, first of all, at what they value most. Clear values reach beyond PCC decisions about money. They serve to open the eyes of local churches to the sending love of God. They work to slow down activists and speed up armchair theologians, and for this reason alone they are priceless stepping-stones for a mission-shaped Church.[8]

A parish church that prays through its mission values, teaches them, makes them its own in the light of the word of God and of the holy sacraments – such a church will then be in a good place to ask the right questions. And for those doing mission in an anxious age, asking the wrong questions will sink you at the start.

But what sort of questions should the parish church be asking?

Knowing and telling; the ticking clock and the clock face

What goes to make up a clock? Just about anything – sand, water, sunshine, springs, gears, quartz crystals, gold, silver, plastic, steel. Yet underneath all the diversity, every clock has two essential components. One is the bit that *knows* the time – the mechanism, the bit that makes the clock tick. The other is the bit that *tells* the time – digital numbers, a sundial arm, a voice, hands on a dial – in short a clock face, the bit that you need to see or hear. Any clock needs both components, a mechanism and a face. Otherwise it will either not be right, or it won't be helpful.

In local church life also there are two essential components – the bit that *knows* the good news for its community, and the bit that *tells* the good news to its community. And in church planning, each component is built by asking questions: either questions that tick, or clock-face questions.

Now *Mission-shaped Church* is full of excellent stories and examples of fresh expressions of church. If you visit the 'Fresh Expressions' website[9] you will find hundreds more, with new ones added every day. It's possible for creative and committed church people to read these, get excited by them, and very quickly begin to ask questions such as these:

- Should we have a café church in our parish?

- What about a nightclub church?

- Or an Internet church for young people?

- Or a church for new-age seekers?

- Or a church in the school?

These are excellent questions, and they need answers. *Mission-shaped Church* is written to help with those answers, and to show churches how to find their own. But all the questions above are clock-face questions. They ask about the Church, and the shape of the Church for mission.

By themselves the questions above are not questions about a mission-shaped Church. In Professor John Hull's words, they are questions about how we can best do church-shaped mission.[10] And despite some misunderstandings about this, *Mission-shaped Church* really is saying that if the Church is truly to be a Church shaped for mission, clock-face questions must come second. The questions that tick must come first. And the mission clock ticks in time with what God is doing in his world.

Questions that tick behind the clock face will be questions such as these:

- Why are the elderly people around here unable to afford a cup of tea in the café?
  (or Why has the local café closed? or Why don't our elderly people want to have a cup of tea in McDonald's?)

- Why do the streets round our nightclub have a binge-drinking problem?
  (or Why don't we have a nightclub? or Why do the young people of our village binge-drink on the village green?)

- How old are the people in our parish who want to use the Internet and can't?

- Why is *The Da Vinci Code* the best-selling book in our local bookshop? What do those who bought it say about it?

- What are the school governors going to do about government plans for extended school hours?

These questions pay close attention to the world as it is. Many of them are questions revolving around the building up, or the tearing down, of social capital.[11] They concern human flourishing, human togetherness and human exclusion. These are deeply traditional questions for the Church; in the second century Irenaeus said, 'The glory of God is humanity fully alive; and the life of human beings is in the vision of God.'[12] And they are also questions that can give rise to some surprising answers for a Christian community, if they are followed through with courage. They can give rise to churches that look like nothing we would even begin to understand as church today. That's one surprise. Another surprise is that they can lead us to develop a church life that looks, and on the outside is, no different from what we already have in our parish. Or maybe they will lead to parallel expressions of church within the one parish, circuit or deanery.

Asking the questions that tick: Dudley Wood

St John the Evangelist serves the parish of Dudley Wood in the Black Country. Its priest-in-charge Judith Oliver led a 'Theology Fun Day' aimed at asking the questions that tick.

'We divided into groups and played a customized board game, with counters and "People Cards" and "Resource Cards" and dice. The game was about matching situations and people's needs against what we either do, or could, offer to our community. The product of the exercise was in the first instance responses written up on Graffiti Walls, and then after lunch getting creative with glue and sticky paper, tissue and pens to create our "dream scenario" for our church . . . Here are some of the responses we had, from participants aged from 5 to 80+:

Isn't it a shame that . . .

● Our resources are limited

● People are scared of coming to church

● Some people don't have a garden

- Some people spoil the parks with broken glass
- Some people give up on church so easily
- People are dying from cancer

Isn't it good that . . .

- We are all friends at church
- We have a church hall to hire
- We have lots of green space
- We have a 'Coffee Stop' every Friday morning
- Our church is fun
- We have a great jumble sale
- We introduced ourselves to the new people on the Speedway housing development

Wouldn't it be good if . . .

- There were details about the church hall on a notice board
- We had a garden where people could see, smell, taste and watch
- There were no wars
- We advertised our 'calendar of events'
- We had better links with the Local Authority to offer things in partnership (eg promoting healthy living)
- We contacted Social Services to ask about working together to provide events for eg people with learning difficulties
- We advertised in the Post Office.'

Any local church with mission-centred values at its heart will ask these kinds of question. And if the questions emerge from values and from the vision of God, then the local church will be prepared to put its own shape in the melting pot to develop an answer to them.

Questions with an edge: the clock is ticking

Much of this is really good and reassuring news for those of us who have spent years nourished by traditional forms of church life, and who are fashioning those forms to touch people today. If life is built on values it will not always involve frantic change. And if change is built on values it will not be frantic, and it will never happen for its own sake. In his book *Emergingchurch.info*, Michael Moynagh writes that *Mission-shaped Church* is 'not about meteors crushing dinosaurs'[13] – in other words, it's not about lots of smart new ideas squashing everything we have now by taking for granted that it's useless and out of date. And Bob Jackson makes the wise distinction between a *bright* idea and a *good* idea.[14]

Not change for change's sake, then. It's much more challenging than that. To build a parish church's life on mission values is not just to change the look of it. It is to change everything.

An anxious church is beset by initiatives. Mission committees have them; clergy have them; bishops have them; the national church has them. Wise church people have learned to spot initiatives gathering in the distance, like storm clouds. And like those who live in the hurricane belt in the southern USA, the response is automatic: keep your head down and wait until it passes. Retreat to the 'storm room' in the middle of your house, take a deep breath, get on with life, and eventually things will calm down.

If you have this reflex, you might be tempted to see all this talk of values and vision as an excuse not to ask questions at all. 'Oh, yes, we thought so. Everything we do is possibly – no, probably – mission after all. No need for any trendy stuff. The status quo *is* the way forward.' That way of thinking flows from initiative-fatigue. It is understandable, but it is mistaken. To assume that the Church can ask questions of the world, but that these questions will not radically affect the Church's own common life, is simply wrong. It too is a clock-face response, a Church-shaped response, but this time what's ticking behind it is a time bomb.

The people of this nation are deeply interested in spirituality and in eternal questions, and want to know how those questions can shape their lives. But when they reach out to learn and discover about God, it seems that they will not and cannot reach the Church.

And yet Christians are called to be with people where they are, with the love of God in Jesus Christ. If we are out of people's reach, we need to be moving, and frankly we need to be getting a move on.

The mission of God is the mother of the Church. If this is so, then anxious twitching is not the answer. Rearranging the furniture on the *Titanic* is not the answer. Living in the storm room is not the answer. But if it's the mission of God, then the good news is that there will be an answer. It will not be a generalized answer. It will not necessarily be a trendy answer. It will not be prescribed by reports or experts. It will be revealed by God to local churches who live out mission values and ask mission questions.

2 That was then ... a Church built on mission values

Paul Bayes

The last chapter looked at the importance of values as a foundation for the shape of the Church. Later we'll look at how this plays out in the everyday working experience of parish churches today. Here I put together a few snapshots of the Church in England – sepia photographs from our past – as a way of remembering that our mission-shaped Church has always had a mission-shaped history.

Assenting to mission

> The Church of England is part of the One, Holy, Catholic and Apostolic Church, worshipping the one true God, Father, Son and Holy Spirit. It professes the faith uniquely revealed in the Holy Scriptures and set forth in the catholic creeds, which faith the Church is called upon to proclaim afresh in each generation. Led by the Holy Spirit, it has borne witness to Christian truth.[1]

The preface to the Declaration of Assent is a pretty robust statement. It speaks with pride and clarity of the inheritance of faith, and it clearly calls the Church to a fresh expression of this inheritance 'in each generation'. In an age when the Anglican tradition struggles to achieve credibility in the eyes of the world, and increasingly in the eyes of many of its own people, it's good to remember that at its heart *Mission-shaped Church* is simply recalling us to our own foundations.

One of those foundations has always been an openness to what God is doing in other parts of the world and the Church. Thus a lot of the inspiration for new ways of being church has come from outside England and outside the Anglican family – Cell Church from new churches in Singapore, West Africa and Texas; Base Ecclesial Communities from Roman Catholic Latin America; Seeker Church from Chicago; new monastic communities from the European mainland. All this richness is informing and strengthening the Church here. But the preface to the Declaration of Assent proclaims that the shape of the Church in England was fashioned before and after the Reformation on a base of mission values, and should be honoured and developed as such.

Emerging church, emerging parish: Theodore of Tarsus

There will never be a TV crime series about a detective who gets on with his or her bosses and does things by the book. Postmodern society has a great love for individualists, mavericks, those who operate in curves and loops and disregard structures. This is one reason why today's Church loves the idea of Celtic Christianity so much, and why so many of our popular saints are courageous oddballs – more like Columbo or Morse than *Yes, Minister* and Sir Humphrey Appleby.

This culture finds it hard to like straight-line people, whose calling is to set up structures and produce order. It's hard to bless them; easier to call them control freaks. And yet some of the most influential mission leaders of the Church have been people like that – such as St Boniface, the greatest mission bishop England has ever sent out.

But England also received its own straight-line mission bishop in Theodore of Tarsus. In AD 668 Pope Vitalian consecrated the 65-year-old Theodore as the eighth Archbishop of Canterbury and sent him to England, where he began to get things organized. As Bede puts it, he was 'the first Archbishop whom all the English obeyed'[2] (and indeed he may well have been the last . . .). By 671 he was calling a Synod to sort out the date of Easter, clarify marriage law, establish codes of conduct for the clergy, and firm up diocesan structures. And throughout his subsequent episcopate, building on all this, he is credited with laying the foundations of the parish system.

I'm claiming Theodore as a mission-shaped saint because he listened to his culture. In planning as he did he was building on the emerging human reality of the region, township or village. These new communities demanded, and were receiving, legal government. By imagining a nation where the Church's systems worked over the same ground as the emerging local government, Theodore and his colleagues and successors used their cultural context as a vessel for the mission of the Church.

Even straight-line people and systems can be flexible and responsive. In his book *Parochial Vision*[3] Nick Spencer underlines just how fluid the parish system was in the five hundred years after Theodore. The Church responded both to a fast-changing political world and to the initiatives and personalities of its own leaders by producing mission-shaped groupings: minsters and their satellites, interdependent communities of faith – indeed, many of the initiatives that the Church has been reinventing and testing in the twentieth and twenty-first centuries, and quite a few of the church-planting models that *Mission-shaped Church* recommends.

Thus the parish system of England, which was in place at the birth of the Anglican movement, was a mission response to the cultures of its day. And in holding fast to the parish system as part of its life, the Church of England has built on a mission foundation.

Commitment to the parish system is commitment to mission; there is no theological room in it for the idea that the Church is just there to chaplain its own. Of course this runs the risks of complacency and of blithely assuming that all English people are Anglican Christians at heart. Even when this was legally enforceable it was never true; and the insult and pain that this arrogant assumption has given to other Christian families is well known and deplorable. All the same, there is no doubt that as a mission narrative the parish system has served the Church of England well. We build on it still, and we should.

Transforming society in the image of the kingdom: the Clapham Sect

In the late 1700s and early 1800s Clapham was a pleasant village separated from London by three miles of countryside. Its vicar, Henry Venn, had recently rebuilt the parish church. From 1792 onwards Venn's son John became vicar. And in that year a group of people, most of them involved in public life, began to make this village and its church their base, and many of them made it their home.

The way these particular people lived, the combination of friendship and discipleship in their community, attracted as much attention as the things they sought to do politically. A whole-life gospel was being attempted, and people noticed.

Not all the attention was positive. Some, looking at this fresh expression of Christian community, felt distaste and contempt for 'that patent Christianity which has been for some time manufacturing at Clapham'[4] and bestowed on the friends the name 'Clapham Sect'.

The political influence of William Wilberforce and his friends and colleagues, and their eventual success in abolishing the slave trade act, is well known. But the members of the Clapham Sect demonstrate the mission values of the Church of England precisely because their focus on holiness and the vision of God issued in two things: social transformation, and a new way of expressing church life.

It is said of Henry Thornton, the guiding spirit of the Clapham Sect, that he set three hours aside each day in the midst of his busy public life for private prayer. Although this may seem remarkable now, it was not so in the eyes of the Sect's contemporaries. What they found remarkable was the picture of a relaxed, cultured, cheerful group of people, living in and out of one another's homes and sharing their lives in common, and out of this forging the ties of friendship and commitment which made them such a force politically.

The famous description of the believers in the second chapter of Acts catches exactly the slightly bewildered attitude of the world to any fresh expression of church:

> All who believed were together and had all things in common; they would sell their possessions and goods and distribute the proceeds to all, as any had need. Day by day, as they spent much time together in the temple, they broke bread at home and ate their food with glad and generous hearts, praising God and having the goodwill of all the people. And day by day the Lord added to their number those who were being saved. (Acts 2.44-47, NRSV)

And the same bewilderment greeted the Clapham Sect:

> Others of the group visited and lived with their co-labourers . . . with an easy informality which seems almost incredible in this day.[5]

> They treated each other's homes as their own . . . kept together for their holidays and while in London arranged to meet for breakfast or dinner to discuss their many common concerns.[6]

> They lived not as nuclear families, but as a family of families.[7]

It is always a mistake to read the present from the face of the past. The Clapham Sect was a creature of its time, wholly in keeping with the social and class culture of the (mostly privileged) people who constituted it. All the same it is not far-fetched to see the Sect as a fresh expression of church. In fact, despite the name others gave it, and its open and ecumenical spirit, it was not a sect in any sense. Almost all its members were faithful Anglicans. Many of them worshipped regularly at Clapham parish church and were spiritually nourished and fed through John Venn's ministry as vicar there. But the lifestyle, 'a family of families', stretched far beyond Sunday, and far beyond formal church worship, and far beyond Clapham, and included and embraced people whose homes and places of work were many miles away. Thus Wilberforce could write to Venn from a friend's home: 'We are here in full force and I should be ashamed of pouring thus into a friend's house en masse, if I were not really conscious that I should like to receive, as well as to pay, such a visit.'[8]

In the language of *Mission-shaped Church*, the Clapham Sect was an associational network, made real by hospitality, a shared commitment to justice, and what Bonhoeffer came to call the 'secret discipline' of the Christian life. As such it was profoundly counter-cultural, and as a lifestyle it astonished those who knew of it. And yet the fruit of such an expression of church is to be counted not in terms of creative church life but in terms of the transformation of society. And as such it is world-famous.

The gift of small groups: John Wesley, classes and bands

> 'I am Jones, looking for something to eat.'
> (William Temple, after being accused of watering down the faith, and of always asking 'What will Jones swallow?')

In 1701 Samuel Wesley began to meet with eight other people in his home at Epworth Rectory in order to 'First, pray to God; Secondly, to read the

Holy Scriptures, and discourse upon Religious Matters for their mutual edification; And Thirdly, to deliberate about the Edification of our neighbour, and the promoting of it.'[9] Two years later his son John was born.

Universities have always been great places for experiment and intensity, and seedbeds for all kinds of clubs, groups and societies, as young people seek to grow and make sense of their lives. So it was that when Charles Wesley founded the 'Holy Club' at Oxford he was not trying to set up a structure for renewing the Church. His focus was much more personal: to find out what it might mean to live the Christian life seriously. His brother John, who became involved in the Holy Club from 1726, remembering the example of his own father, had the same motivation. Within a year the Club had become a place of Bible study and prayer, and also a place of practical Christian action (visiting prisoners and the sick) and personal and sacramental accountability. It too was a fresh expression of church.

Although he was ordained when he became leader of the 'Holy Club', it was to be another nine years before John's heart was 'strangely warmed' in May 1738. Thus small groups in Methodism began, not as a bright management idea, but as the sharing and imparting of a way of living that had transformed the Wesleys themselves – 'I am Jones, looking for something to eat'.

Even so, it took Wesley a while to grasp the power of what he himself had lived out. In Bristol in 1742, an enterprising leader arranged to visit a dozen people in order to collect their financial contribution to the chapel. By doing this regularly, he discovered that he was able to keep a finger on the pulse of their lives. They had the chance to share their Christian journey, in a way that Sunday contacts could never provide. He passed on this news to Wesley, who later reflected: 'It struck me immediately, this is the very thing we have wanted so long.'[10] From this regular contact, and the accountability it brought, the class and band system grew.

Wesleyan theology makes much of the prevenient grace of God, drawing the seeker on to the point of commitment and regeneration. Flowing from this, their small group system was threefold, from the 'trial bands' for sincere enquirers (4–6 people with a leader), through to the 'classes' (up to 36 people) for those who had made a commitment to Christ and wanted to know more, and the 'bands' (just 4–8 people) for discipled believers who wanted to grow more fully into God's grace.[11] Attendance at their class was a requirement for the people called Methodists; attendance at the band, an option for those wanting to live more deeply. 'The focus of the class meeting is the mind; the band meeting focuses on the will.'[12] In early US Methodism about 20 per cent of the believers were in bands; and as their leader, Bishop Francis Asbury, said, 'Where the bands flourish, Methodism flourishes.'

For Wesley the numbers of people attending preaching meetings was not significant. What mattered for the new Methodist societies was the numbers involved in the classes. And about this he was meticulous, and he could be rightly scathing about the tendency of leaders to inflate attendance figures.

No formal manual for band leaders was ever written in the Wesleys' lifetime, beyond the 'Rules' below. This is partly because the leading of a Wesleyan band was such a simple thing, and partly because the nature of the revival meant that many of the band leaders were illiterate. In 1744 the 'Rules for Bands' laid out this simplicity:

We intend:

1. To meet once a week, at the least.

2. To come punctually at the hour appointed, without some extraordinary reason.

3. To begin (those of us who are present) exactly at the hour, with singing or prayer.

4. To speak each of us in order, freely and plainly, the true state of our souls, with the faults we have committed in thought, word, or deed, and the temptations we have felt since our last meeting.

5. To end every meeting with prayer suited to the state of each person present.

6. To desire some person among us to speak his own state first, and then to ask the rest, in order, as many and as searching questions as may be, concerning their state, sins, and temptations.[13]

And at every meeting just five questions were always asked:

1. What known sins have you committed since our last meeting?

2. What temptations have you met with?

3. How were you delivered?

4. What have you thought, said, or done, of which you doubt whether it be sin or not?

5. Have you nothing you desire to keep secret?

Not complicated, then; just difficult. Band meetings were not cult-like; on the contrary they were easy to leave and hard to join. With a sharp eye on quality control, Wesley was far more likely to expel existing members than to press-gang new ones. Moreover, in England, they relied on regular sacramental attendance at the parish church to round out a fully discipled Christian life.

This is tough and strange stuff. Wesley's authoritarian streak made regular membership essential, and to miss a couple of meetings was to risk expulsion. The bands were segregated by gender and marital status, so that they were genuinely peer-group meetings. The ferocity of their discipline, within a movement which tried so hard to remain part of the established church, may seem odd and over-intense to us. But for all their strangeness, the methods of the Methodists grew Christians quickly, and they did so among working-class communities where literacy was low and where, as a rule, Anglican commitment was vanishingly weak. They managed to empower people, and to build leadership and peer accountability, in ways that today's Church has not yet managed to approach.

Partly because of the high demands they made on people, in the fullness of time in Methodism the bands were the first to go; the class meetings became more intellectual and lasted longer, a change that came to its fullest flowering in the US adult Sunday-school movement.

But the Wesleys' desire as students to be serious disciples of Jesus Christ, and their organizational ability, gave us the pattern of the small group network – perhaps the very greatest gift from English Christians to the world Church.

Mission in a changing context:
Charles Lowder and Charles Blomfield

> There was dissension in the parish. A Mr Westerton opposed
> the high-church practices and sought election as church-
> warden in order to end them. To this purpose he hired a man
> to perambulate the area carrying a sandwich board
> proclaiming the message, 'Vote Westerton'. Mr Lowder, in
> what he described later as 'a moment of madness', gave some
> of the choir boys 6d with which to purchase rotten eggs, and
> so armed, they assaulted the poor board carrier. Mr Lowder
> appeared before Westminster Magistrates where he was fined
> £2, and before the Bishop of London, who suspended him
> from duty for six weeks.[14]

Stories like this make Anglican squabbles seem much less fun than they used
to be. The incident of the eggs took place during Charles Lowder's curacy in
Pimlico. Despite this sulphurous beginning, he went on to become one of
the greatest of the East End slum priests. On the other hand Charles
Blomfield, the bishop who suspended him, is rather grimly remembered as a
straight-line man, heir to the spirit of Theodore of Tarsus. According to
legend Blomfield was privately amused by Lowder's crime, referring to it
with a classicist's wit as 'Lowder's ovation'. But in public, and probably in fact,
the attitudes of the two men were poles apart. In their very different ways,
however, they were creative and innovative in their approach to the wholly
new problems of the Victorian city. A mission-shaped Church grounded in
worship was central to the vision of both.

Charles Lowder: the mass and the masses

By suspending him, Bishop Blomfield refocused Lowder's life. Lowder spent
his six weeks' suspension in France where he was so inspired by the
example of St Vincent de Paul that he returned to England wholly convinced
that the face of Christ was to be seen in the Eucharist and in the poor. This
focus informed and invested his work in East London, and in London Docks
in particular.

Anglican Catholicism has earned its reputation for ordered beauty and glory. One of the lessons of the growth of Catholic mission parishes in East London through the later nineteenth century was precisely this offering of colour, beauty and holiness in a social context which lacked all three. So a ritualist church was shaping itself for mission. All the same, in looking at what it meant for Lowder to be a mission priest, it's important to get an unsentimental flavour of what mission-church worship was like in fact. Far from being aesthetic, head-in-the-clouds stuff, this was worship that confronted the spirit of the East London slums directly and often violently:

> Mission sermons were preached on the streets, Evensong
> sung, somewhat roughly in the house. The sermons were
> interspersed with cat-calls, dancing groups of prostitutes, and
> the throwing of stones, human excrement and once a dead
> cat. The missioners persisted; in August 1856 Mr Lowder
> moved to Wapping, rented a dilapidated house in Calvert
> Street and named the new church plant 'The Good Shepherd
> Mission'.[15]

In 1866, on the day after the newly built St Peter's, London Docks, was opened, a case of cholera was discovered. The subsequent epidemic ravaged the East End. Lowder and his colleagues put their lives at risk to help the sick, and in the same period began the daily Mass in the Good Shepherd Chapel of the new parish church. After the epidemic he became known as 'Father Lowder', a title given not by his congregation, but by his parish.

For Lowder's community to hold fast to the real presence of Christ in these increasingly secularized circumstances was for them to do church in a new way. It demanded exactly the kind of spiritual discipline that *Mission-shaped Church* advocates for today.[16] Worship and mission have never been separable. In Lowder and his colleagues the East End Catholic tradition held to this truth and discovered this reality: common life and mutual accountability, fed from and centred on worship, issuing in action for healing and justice.

Charles Blomfield: building the Church, building the churches

> Anglican church-extension ... was always a hopeful rather
> than a rational activity.[17]

Blomfield shaped the mission of his diocese in a different way, a bricks-and-mortar way. Responding to the explosion in the population of his diocese, in his years as Bishop of London he consecrated around 200 new church buildings. Not everyone thanked him for this at the time, and not everyone thanks him now. The Vicar of Hyde Park, losing three thousand of his wealthy parishioners to the new benefice of All Saints, Norfolk Square, complained bitterly that pew rents worth £877 (over £40,000 in today's money) had been lost to him. And for some London Anglicans today, facing expensive repairs to their churches, Blomfield's church-building drive feels like a wretched millstone. 'Working on the principle that if you open more pubs you sell more beer, [Blomfield] could not know that the decline in belief would leave many churches empty and unwanted.'[18]

And yet in London over 150 years ago, Blomfield built churches in hope and expectation, basing himself on the value of worship at the heart of a missionary Church.

Today London Diocese is growing. In his 2005 book *The Road to Growth*, Bob Jackson sees it as a flagship example of what a mission diocese can be: 'the Diocese of London has been in significant numerical growth since the early 1990s and it is still continuing'.[19] This has happened in the midst of all those church buildings, including Blomfield's buildings. Planting and transplanting is blessed in the diocese, and it normally makes use of existing church buildings: 'The policy in regard to churches in danger of closure is to invite a team in from another church to revive them. This has been enormously successful.'[20]

Of course Charles Blomfield did not have all this in mind when he embarked on his church-building drive. Nor did he use the language of mission values. Nonetheless he built with those values as well as with bricks, mortar and fundraising committees. His purpose was to see God worshipped and the people of London served in the name of Christ. As the quote at the head of this section implies, his hopes may have been irrational; but God seems to be fulfilling them just the same.

Today Bishop Blomfield is not widely seen as a mission hero. Perhaps this is a pity. Certainly T. S. Eliot saw him as such in his poem 'The Rock' – Blomfield 'who built in a time which was no better than this'.

This chapter has been trying to look at familiar examples of our life as Christians in England through the lens of mission. The local history of your own parish, area or diocese will almost certainly offer many more examples, and by finding and repeating these you might wish to help your own community step out more proudly as a church with a history shaped by God's mission. So, for example, the Diocese of Salisbury reclaimed one of its founding fathers, St Aldhelm, as a mission inspiration:

> Aldhelm lived in the seventh century. In the twelfth century William of Malmesbury wrote: 'During his time as Abbot, Aldhelm noticed that instead of attending to the monks at Mass, the local people preferred to spend their time gossiping and could not be persuaded to listen to the preacher. So one day, he stationed himself on a bridge, like a minstrel, and began to sing his ballads. The beauty of his verse attracted a huge crowd and, when he had caught their attention, he began to preach the gospel.'

The diocese continued:

> Now, celebrating Aldhelm's 1300th Anniversary and the 'Aldhelm Way' of making new disciples challenges us to think of new ways of putting Jesus' commandments into practice and fulfilling our mission as Christians. Aldhelm's anniversary in 2005 provides the opportunity to think creatively about new events and activities through which we might grow as the body of Christ and serve our local communities.[21]

'Behold, I make all things new' (Revelation 21.5). The creativity that the Lord brings by his Spirit can cause mission-shaped parish churches to flourish in this millennium also. In the rest of this book we'll try to identify areas where that is happening, and can happen. That was then ... But what about now?

3 Mission-shaped worship
Tim Sledge

We are arguing that 'mission' should never be the icing on the cake of the Church, but central to every aspect of its life. What does it mean, then, to apply the mission values to the bread-and-butter work of the parish church? Weekly worship, for example? This chapter explores that question.

story
story
story
story

In St Boniface PCC consideration was being given to the follow-up from an evangelistic occasion the previous week. The most obvious response was to invite people to the Sunday worship a couple of days later to hear a presentation of the Christian faith and to see the church family in worship. As the group responded to this suggestion there was widespread hesitation followed by an honest admission from one member: 'Well, I am not sure I would want to invite anyone to what we do on Sunday – it might put them off.'

This is not an uncommon admission. The truth is that if worship isn't interesting, attractive and conveying something of the glory of God to those inside the Church, then the mission of God will certainly be impaired. How can our services of worship engage both with those who attend regularly and with those who are new to the whole experience?

> Sometimes I sit in church and think this is absolute rubbish, sometimes I sit in church and think this is all that matters.[1]

> If I don't worship, I will shrivel and die.[2]

> The revitalization of worship is high on the church's agenda . . . How can we have the kind of worship to which we are not embarrassed to bring our friends and partners? Indeed, how can we have the kind of worship that may expose others to an experience of God?[3]

Losing our mains connection

> Worship lies at the heart of a missionary church, and to love
> and know God as Father, Son and Holy Spirit is its chief
> inspiration and primary purpose.[4]

Different church traditions approach the whole gospel of God in different
ways. There's no doubt that for the vast majority of the Church of England,
worship is the essential starting point for all our doctrine and all our activity.
Historically, Anglicans have found in their worship the locus of their belief
and practice, their being and their living. And not only Anglicans, as the
Scottish/Westminster Catechism famously says in answer to the question
'Why were you created?', it is 'To worship God and enjoy him for ever.'

If this is why we were created, then it is always right that our personal and
corporate worship should be at the top of all agendas. And it's natural that
resting in the truth and reality of God is the 'first among equals' of the values
outlined in *Mission-shaped Church*:

> To make evangelism the primary concern of the church is to
> give it a misplaced and exaggerated position in our lives. The
> first task of the church is to worship.[5]

The Church should derive its power to convert from its worship. When
worship fulfils its purpose, we connect with God, with ourselves and with
other people in a way that is life-transforming. 'Doxology is the heartbeat
of mission.'[6]

And yet we must be honest. Many of us may pour our hearts into the
leading and preparation of excellent worship, but we are nonetheless losing
connection with many people who feel that the worship which is offered in
their local parish church does not speak to their spiritual condition.

> story
> story
> story
> story
>
> A 'dechurched' enquirer was talking recently about his journey back to faith after 20 years. After a while, the question of where to worship came up. The key criterion for this person was not the style of service nor the distance to travel. Instead he said, 'I want something which is going to connect me with the living God. I don't care what that looks like – I don't mind being challenged or even uncomfortable – but where can I go in my area that is going to work for me?'

This seeker was talking about a place where he could make connections. Of course there are many such who have found a home within each local church. But there are also a significant number whose relationship with the Church has been lost (cf. the Preface, pp. ix-x). These are people who no longer see a relevance to their lives in the worship of the Church. And along with the many who have voted with their feet, there are many more who are in our churches week by week and would rather not be there; they come simply out of duty.

These facts will cripple a mission-shaped church. Are we really going to invite people to something that we find uninspiring ourselves? In a recent survey of people who had either left church or were on the edge,[7] many spoke of the lack of connectedness between their lives and the Church's teaching and preaching, and of their longing for a spirituality to resource and inspire. Their frustrations point us again to the need for worship to be rooted in the values of mission. Worship has a key part to play in accompanying people into the reality of God. Worship helps to make connections.[8]

As we survey the worship of our church from the viewpoint of mission we see dysfunction. On the one hand there is evidence of frustration and unmet need and on the other an unhealthy reaction, a commitment from many who lead and design worship to protect and preserve their inheritance regardless: 'Why should we care about bums on seats?' 'Our worship is for God alone; others will see that eventually, and if they don't it's their problem.' What is at the heart of this mismatch? Within a complex picture we believe there are two key factors: fear of change, and the loss of successful engagement with today's culture.

Fear of change

> In *one single day* in 2005, there was as much trade as during
> the whole of the year of 1949, as much scientific research as
> during the whole of 1960, as many telephone calls as during
> the whole of 1983 and as many emails as during the whole of
> 1990.[9]

A primary cause of our loss of connection is the speed of cultural and social
change and the defensive reactions and fear this calls forth from the Church.
So much of what we hold on to as part of the familiar landscape seems to
be eroding away. It is hard to keep track of the speed of change in life. Many
Christians have ceased to engage with with the world, and cling to 'my
worship, my familiar words' like a piece of driftwood running down the
rapids of cultural change. Compulsively we hang on to what we know, so
that we don't drown in the rapids. Called to celebrate and worship an
unchanging and immense God, we are reduced to worshipping a small God
in a way that never changes.

> Part of the difficulty the church faces in persuading people of
> an inquiring mind that there is a place for them within it arises
> because of the apparent fixity of our symbolical systems . . .
> [churches] are nostalgic havens from incessant change; they
> represent the best of what we have been or imagined
> ourselves to be.[10]

'I might not be able to find the cornflakes in the supermarket any more and
I get lost because they have changed the layout of the roads again, but at
least I know what I am going to get on a Sunday morning. At least there are
some constants in my life and I don't want them to change – in fact if they
go I will be completely lost.' This fearful and nostalgic spirit can pervade the
long-term core of a congregation. In resisting liturgical change the unspoken
feeling, from frightened believers of all ages, becomes, 'Well, as long as this
service sees me out of this church in a box then I don't mind'. Of course
this is an unkind overstatement, but it points sharply to the gap between the
motive of much worship and the values of the God of mission.

As a member of one rural church in the south Midlands said:

> Tomorrow the children are doing something about Jonah and
> the whale with a large sheet of blue plastic. I don't mind
> going, but some people in the church are staying away
> because they don't like that sort of thing in church.

The frequency of this sort of reaction to innovation can lead to the sad but inevitable conclusion that many churchgoers remain connected to their pattern of worship at the expense of accessibility to those outside the Church. Of course sheets of blue plastic will not necessarily lead people to God. But at the level of values the underlying attitude being expressed is: 'If you want to come to church, come on our terms and fit in with our style of worship – you are not welcome here unless you conform to our way of doing things.' And of course the cost of this, our understandable but ultimately misplaced fear of change, is that we have lost touch with the communities of unchurched around us.

Losing touch with today's culture

> To some Christians, the idea of inviting our . . . friends to
> worship with us is highly problematic. It could be
> embarrassing. The worship services in many of our churches
> are often either so uninspiring and clannish, or so unintelligent
> and unintelligible – or both – that we'd rather not invite
> others. If that is the case, we have a real problem on our
> hands. Many churches have now recognized the seriousness of
> the situation. The revitalization of worship is high on the
> church's agenda . . . How can we have the kind of worship to
> which we are not embarrassed to bring our friends and
> partners? Indeed, how can we have the kind of worship that
> may expose others to an experience of God? [11]

Recently a group of regular worshippers from a number of churches was drawn together to share their experiences of worship. One of the questions posed was: 'If you could describe your experience in your church worship as a colour, what colour would that be?' The vast majority of responses to the question was 'Grey!'

Meanwhile the world is multi-coloured. The way people learn, process and assimilate information has changed, and continues to change, at a bewildering pace. We live in a visual world, and we process much more visually and aurally than used to be the case. This spoken/seen/moving culture, moving on from a static world of books, reading and still pictures, has been called the 'second orality'. Banks of TV screens with fast-moving images communicate where bill boards with a single statement used to stand. As our method of communication has changed, so also has our expectation of what we receive from organizations. Expectations of quality and customer care have risen exponentially in recent years. Increasingly we demand that large organizations, from the Government to Marks & Spencer, should invest a huge amount in listening to people, responding to need, seeking to reflect customer demand. How has the worshipping church risen to this challenge?

At first it might appear that the Church has been left well and truly behind. If the figures cited earlier are anything to go by, then we are not making the connections we used to. Of course this doesn't mean that we should simply collude with the consumer values of contemporary society. The values of the Church and the Christian faith have always been distinct from the surrounding culture, sometimes sharply distinct; but especially in worship, those distinct values must not be garbled or communicated incomprehensibly.

Rewiring old connections

All of this so far has been a bit gloomy, and indeed rather Victor Meldrew-ish in its complaint. But all is not lost! The values of a worshipping church are not based on style or even substance but on God himself. A value is not driven by what service pattern to use here or there, what language, what sort of songs. The focus is on God, and on the inspiration which God gives to the Church. We are reaching for something which does not collude with the culture or deny it but which is engaging and distinctively different. We are reaching for a worship which makes connections with people and with God.

In the next part of this chapter we will explore how we can pay due attention to the key elements of worship and, by breaking up some of the elements, help shape worship which honours our tradition and engages with our world.

Doing the traditional well

Tradition is the living faith of the dead. Traditionalism is the dead faith of the living.[12]

Tradition is like giving birth, not like wearing your father's hat.[13]

story
story
story
story

On a new estate near Kettering, there has been a church presence for a number of years. At first glance, it would be an ideal place for a church plant or fresh expression of church and there are ongoing discussions regarding cell church. Most of the housing is occupied by young families. Residents commute to various places in the Midlands. The community, while new, is called Mawsley Village. Many have moved there to live a modern recreation of the rural idyll. Over the past two years, the churches have put on local celebrations in the community centre. Most of those who have come to the worship are not part of the church. The Christians there have noticed that when worship is based around a traditional theme such as Harvest or Christingle or Mothering Sunday then numbers have been good – about 70–80 people attend. When there is no 'traditional' festival, then numbers are significantly lower.

This account shows how easily the Christian community can connect with the 'open dechurched' by operating effectively in traditional mode.

In the face of the gloomy picture we've painted above, some critics have written off the established church entirely, saying that the gap between the Church and the world is too great. For them traditional models of church and worship are no longer relevant to anyone and can never adapt to the local context and culture where they are placed. As we say in our preface, this is certainly true for a growing part of the population, and the thrust of fresh expressions of church is to address that fact.

But as we minister to a nation in transition, that church in Kettering and many others are finding that the old clothed in fresh ways still has the power to convert. They are finding how to make connections between people in the church and those who are seeking for meaning and faith themselves. Through the door of tradition they are leading people to an enriched worship experience, from the colour grey to a rainbow of colours, emotions and engagement.

The story from Kettering is one of a mixed-economy diversity of approach. Worship is informal but builds strongly on the community network links which exist between people from a similar social background.[14] There are many families with children of the same age as well as a gap to 'younger retired' people of 55 and above who may be more familiar with the traditional Church. And when worship is apt,[15] shaped and offered carefully, many people are open and willing to attend.

This is true more widely than Kettering. The Diocese of Manchester has seen extraordinary success with its 'Back to Church Sunday' initiative. This simple piece of missionary work was begun in Greater Manchester: on one Sunday in September, churches welcome people who, for whatever reason, have lost contact with their local church. Now growing and spreading across the country, the 'Back to Church' initiative has demonstrated that many dechurched people are willing and open to return to church provided they receive encouragement. This comes via personal contact from Christian friends who offer an invitation, confident that the worship they will experience really will make those life connections. As one person, now fully reintegrated into the worshipping community, remarked: 'I had simply forgotten how good and helpful church can be.'

Following the 'Back to Church' initiative, the University of Wolverhampton researched the motivating factors of those who had come, together with their evaluation of what they had liked or disliked. Their outcomes underline that many people are open to return to church: they are low-lying fruit for mission, to be grasped alongside more radical and essential mission initiatives.

This research challenges the assumption that Christendom with its focus on the Church in its inherited mode is dead and gone. There is no doubt that the profile and influence of the traditional Church has faded but for as long as there are still vestiges of awareness in people's lives, there are still opportunities. Moreover the initial connection point for many people is still going to be a service of worship. There is a local pastoral exercise to be done here, re-establishing a culture of invitation and honestly ensuring that the worship which we provide makes connections, honouring our tradition but not being a slave to it.[16] All the work done since the decade of evangelism on 'healthy churches', and the work of popular courses such as 'Leading Your Church Into Growth', remains relevant and useful here.[17]

Making Sunday count

So mission values can be visible in Sunday worship, and churches grow when they do Sunday better. But what are the key ingredients of a worship that is vital and attractive? How are those connections being made which spark recognition of the living God?

Anyone who has worked hard to design and lead effective worship will know that there are no glib quick fixes or overly simplistic solutions to that challenging question. Nevertheless, we do believe that there are some simple principles that can invest all kinds of worship with freshness and life.

Time to prepare

First, there is the issue of preparation time. For parish churches one of the great joys of the Anglican liturgy is that it is a gift from the wider Church. We are the recipients and custodians of a rich heritage of worship variety – of texts and music and accounts of worship – which has been shaped and formed over many years. This does not mean that we can treat it like a microwave ready meal – no preparation and just follow the instructions on the packet and 'Ping!' your worship will come out piping hot and ready to be consumed. Time spent on preparing worship is time well spent. And for a mission-shaped parish, substantial quality time spent thinking creatively and sensitively about the needs of people and the 'connection value' of worship is vital.

Excellence

> My people like mediocrity. They feel threatened by excellence in worship.[18]

In one sense it is obvious to say that when we observe the relevant principles the end result will be excellent worship. However, the word excellence itself needs to be seen in the context of mission values. The danger is that 'excellence' can so often be translated into action as an esoteric event of great beauty and liturgical correctness – which makes little or no connection with the people. Worship 'performed' beautifully from the front, be it by a worship band or a trained choir, can too often turn a congregation of intelligent free-thinking people into passive observers. A key question that those of us who lead and design acts of worship need to ask consistently is how we can turn passive observers into active participants so that everyone is drawn into the experience.

Let's look at some key principles that might help us make those connections between worship and mission, between us and God.

Paying attention to the main elements

> [A]ll, whether they live in the city or the countryside, are gathered together in unity. Then the records of the apostles are read . . . When the reader has concluded, the presider in a discourse admonishes and invites us into the pattern of these good things. Then we stand and offer prayer, . . . And, as we said before, when we have concluded the prayer, bread is set out to eat, together with wine and water. The presider offers up prayer and thanksgiving, as much as he can, and the people sing out their assent saying the Amen. There is distribution . . . Those who are prosperous and desire to do so, give what they wish. [The presider] aids orphans and widows. In short, the presider is a guardian to all those who are in need.[19]

Justin Martyr's description emphasizes key elements of worship which are fully in tune with the values of a mission church. There is the stress on the importance of fellowship and gathering – of that distinctive *koinonia* which is developed more in Chapter 6 on community. But even in AD 150, there is also a recognition of the diversity of background and experiences that people come from and due care is given in this account to building up the body 'in unity'. The emphasis is on worship and discipleship which 'invites us into the pattern of these things'. In other words it seeks to make connection with people's lives. Finally, this is not worship for the insider only; it has the needs of the community at the forefront of its concern. Too often the concern of the Church for justice and human care has been seen as distinct from its worshipping and evangelistic life, and wedges have been driven where they should never be. But here the president is seen as the 'guardian to all those who are in need'. Rereading this passage gives a sense of a narrative told through the worship, a narrative which is clearly running counter to the values of the day, uplifting and strengthening the act of worship itself.

In short, inevitably for a faith based on the revelation of Word made flesh, what emerges from this account is the incarnational value. The two core elements of the incarnation – humanity and divinity – make up what you might call 'The Worship Molecule'.[20] Simple as it is, this diagram can help us refine what we are looking for in worship.

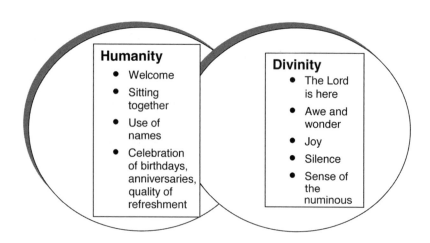

Humanity

Valuing the quality of 'humanity' is recognizing that in corporate worship we are persons in relationship, not isolated individuals in our privatized world. We are different members of a body and need to make the most of opportunities to recognize our shared humanity and celebrate it. A church which is human recognizes this in a number of different ways, each of which embodies the values of the God of mission. Here are a few deceptively simple examples:

- First, welcome – a welcome that is an attitude throughout the church. Welcome is what happens after you have said hello[21] – it's about the people who are open-hearted and thrilled to see new faces and regular ones. It's the spirit of those who take an interest in people for who they are rather than seeing them as a means to some end – especially if the 'end' is church growth.

- A human church is one where people sit together, where the front six pews are not empty and where people don't have 'their own seat' which they have guarded for years and which others touch at their peril. A human church has people who genuinely want to be together.

- A human church recognizes the important rites of passage in people's day-to-day lives. It will weep with the grieving and it will laughingly celebrate with those who laugh. 'Happy Birthday' will be sung as well as 'Let all mortal flesh keep silence'. A human church will not think it vulgar to sing both.

- A human church sees the 'after service care' as an outworking of the worship, as important as the worship itself. Therefore the quality of the coffee, wine or juice will be high (see our Chapter 6 on friendship for more on 'coffee-cup theology').

- Part of celebrating the 'human', living in full awareness of our humanity, is the simple recognition that people have basic needs and are worth investing in. That has consequences for the ambience of the church building.

None of this is rocket science. Imagine that you were inviting friends around for supper in the middle of winter. I guess that you would put the heating on early to ensure that they were comfortable and have everything ready for when they arrived – table laid, house ready for guests. All we need is a similar principle for the church buildings, which are our spiritual homes. Attention to the comfort of people will make a difference. And it's a value thing, not just a growth gimmick. Real, quality attention honours the dignity of our guests – as human beings valued by God. It provides them with a supportive environment to help them enter into worship.

But if the emphasis on humanity is the whole content of our worship then it will certainly deteriorate into 'fireside chat' religion – warm and cosy and frothy with lots of entertainment but lacking any substance. That is why there is a need for the other component of the worship molecule – the one looking to the divinity that the Incarnation reveals.

Divinity

Divinity in worship is about creating a sense of wonder and awe. Divinity is about creating space, worth and expectancy for the living God to dwell in.

There is otherness in worship – the mystery and awe of entering into something that is beyond the usual, which is beautiful, which is holy. A parish church that remembers divinity makes the most of the numinous moments in any worship – such as the confession and absolution. Rather than this just being a few moments of recollecting bad things we have done, it becomes an important and renewing time of reflection and reception of forgiveness. This sense of the moment can be enhanced very effectively with the use of symbols and movement.

story
story
story
story

One church gave everyone a piece of barbed wire and spoke some words of confession as the congregation wrapped a piece of wool on the barbed wire as a sign of their sins and as a reminder of the Lamb of God. These were all offered at the foot of a simple cross and when everyone had placed their barbed wire, each member of the congregation was then given a flower as a sign

> of new life and forgiveness. For many people, it made a
> prayer which they were used to saying almost by rote into a
> living experience of God's forgiveness.

Other ways of remembering 'divinity' in the context of the incarnation include making the most of the rich language, presenting the words dramatically. Sometimes it is too easy to forget the power of the opening words of the Eucharist: 'The Lord is here'. Creative and appropriate use of times of silence and space helps to remind people that this period of encounter with God is of a different order from the outside world.

> One priest was asked by a small child why they had incense in
> the church. The reply: 'Because you can't get it in
> Woolworths.'

This might seem a flippant response, but it contains an important truth. In worship there is always a balance between relevance and reverence; making connections, but being taken out of our routine context into the presence of God where often words are not enough to express the inexpressible.

In an interview, the composer Olivier Messiaen was asked why, in a piano piece depicting the vision of a new heaven and a new earth in Revelation, the music had built to such a climax and intensity and had then suddenly stopped, with a number of ensuing bars of silence. His reply: 'Sometimes in music, even I run out of language to express the glory of God and only silence will do.'[22]

Just as there are many churches that focus on the humanity to the exclusion of the divine and where the line between worship and entertainment is indistinguishably thin, so there are also many churches which focus on the divine to the exclusion of the human. Worship becomes exclusive, so esoteric and focused on the activity of a few people at the front of the church – either robed with an alb or robed with a guitar and microphone. An excellent and beautiful spectacle turns a congregation into onlookers.

So humanity celebrated and the divine adored in worship are the elements that make the spark. And with this spark, worship can be enriched with any number of small (and cost effective!) actions.

Why not stand back and assess the balance between the human and divine in your regular worship, whatever the day of the week? Some churches are fabulous at paying attention to people and the human side of worship. A church will rightly excel in the provision of great cakes, great welcome, great fun and a warm community feel. But is this at the expense of the divine? A church which is nothing but warmth needs substance too. The mission value flowing from the truth of the incarnation never lets us forget that humanity and divinity are not mutually exclusive. An act of worship shaped through the values of mission is worship that is both community-focused *and* triune in its focus also.

In other places it may be that there is a powerful sense of the numinous, the glory and wonder of God expressed through the beauty and care taken in the liturgy; but might this be at the expense of recognizing and making connections with those who are there?

The missional role of *Common Worship*

One of the main criticisms of Anglican worship in the past has been that it lacked the common touch – that it was culturally too fastidious and out of touch with the people. Everything that happens has tended to be focussed on what should happen in the chancel, around the altar and in the pulpit without due consideration of the needs of those in the nave. *Common Worship* has been designed to redress that imbalance. Properly used it is more than a mere collection of service books – it is a treasure trove of resources and variety, with something for pretty much any situation. It has variety and diversity. It is not the complete answer to the issues and challenges we face, but it is an excellent resource to begin to address them.

At the heart of *Common Worship* is a missional way of approaching liturgy, one which is designed to make connections, to enrich and develop our worship – and of course that will look different in different places. The Prayer Book also recognized this missional and pastoral reality. As Cranmer said in the preface to the 1549 *Book of Common Prayer,* 'it often chanceth diversely in diverse counties . . .'. The aim of *The Book of Common Prayer* was that worship should be in the vernacular, readily understandable, so that it could make connections with the lives of the people of the day in order to increase their devotion. Even in the sixteenth century, Cranmer recognized that alongside a desire for regularity was this recognition of a need for diversity in different places.

Sadly, over 400 years later and in spite of all the resources available in *Common Worship* and other authorized texts, there is still a dearth of creativity and variety in many places, which means that the liturgy of Christians does not connect with the communities they serve. To compound the issue, there is often a lack of confidence in using the given liturgies in a dramatic and creative way, which inspires and stimulates mind, soul and body. The hope of *Common Worship* is to offer a permission-granting diversity within a familiar framework. This framework was, and remains, filled with missionary potential, with words and actions waiting to be released and given full value in a world and culture that craves them. With these building blocks the evidence is that vibrant worshipping communities can be built.

Worship as jazz

If we are to remain faithful to the important principle of diversity and use *Common Worship* as a tool for that, our challenge is not to clone but to incarnate. This principle is, of course, at the heart of *Mission-shaped Church*. Professor David Ford helpfully uses jazz as an illustration both for mission and for praise.[23] Jazz, of course, is based both on a central theme and the rich diversity of improvisation. If we extend this analogy to the whole of worship, our core theme becomes the call to worship. It is why we were created. But it is similarly a theme around which diversity and improvisation and variation should flow. Different people playing their own variations at different times provide colour and shade and mood, which are unique to a given place and time. There is individual flair and corporate awareness of each other. What is more, no one jazz performance is identical to the next. The simple fact is that one single tune just won't do!

Jazz is not a mess, but a carefully crafted discipline where different instruments bring out different themes and elaborate on them. Too often in the past in worship, we have tried to put too many ingredients into the same pot. We try to be all things to all people in an hour and a bit on a Sunday morning. To put it mildly this rarely works.

In its place a mission-shaped parish will move towards 'common diversity', developing a varied diet of worship. It is diversity under the one roof. Let's look at some examples of this diversity and content and see how churches have developed their existing members and encouraged new congregations:

story
story
story
story

In the parish of Todmorden, West Yorkshire, there is a *Common Worship* sung Eucharist on the Sunday morning. It is traditional and reflects its core constituency of a traditional Pennine town. The church also has strong links with the local school and, in a desire to build on these links, developed 'Church on Monday'. At 4 p.m. there is a *Common Worship* Eucharist. Many of the elements are similar to Sunday, but much of it, such as the Ministry of the Word, is expressed in a dialect that is appropriate to those who are there.

story
story
story
story

In Peterborough Cathedral, a new service on Saturday afternoons was developed for those enquiring about the Christian faith. It was a recognizable Eucharist, but simply expressed in different ways. The liturgy follows the *Common Worship* format, there are a variety of formal and informal songs and the building is used fully as the congregation process from sharing around the Table of the Word to sharing around the altar.

Neither of these new worship opportunities takes place on a Sunday. One of the themes of our postmodern jazz will be to recognize the 24/7 way that lives are led. About five years ago, the census figures revealed that 30 per cent of the working adult population worked either part time or full time on a Sunday. In the face of that we need to explore a diversity of worship opportunities on different days at different times – appropriate to the life-shapes of those we want to serve.

Do these services and worshipping congregations come under the umbrella of Fresh Expressions? Well, as Archbishop Rowan has said, 'Let's wait and see.' They are fresh expressions of Christian community, but they are rooted in the traditional inherited liturgy of the Church of England – distinct from, say, a café church or a toddler service.

However these ways of worshipping are defined – and they stand for many up and down the country – they demonstrate life in the Church of England, which has been prepared in a way that helps people currently outside the Church to encounter the living God.

Trad jazz

The great thing about focusing on values is that it frees us from a constant pressure to look original. Originality in worship is vital in many places, but others are following the values of mission to old and familiar places. Take, for example, the small but significant number of churches that are thinking creatively around the use of the 1662 Prayer Book.

There are still many people who were brought up on the language of Cranmer's book, to which they are deeply connected and devoted. Sadly, among mission-minded Anglicans 1662 is often seen as the poor relation – often provided for a few people at an inconvenient time of day. But the Prayer Book can also be seen as a living resource, not as a fossilized liturgy. Perhaps 'the 8 o'clock' needs redeeming and to be viewed as a key contributor to the diversity of worshipping opportunities. And indeed a growing number of churches have developed '1662' as a new way of doing church.

story
story
story
story

In Bradford at St Augustine's, the Sunday worship had developed as more of a family service with a non-eucharistic pattern. There was an increasing awareness of a group of people who either used to come to 1662 Communion or knew this pattern of worship from their childhood. The church started a mid-week 1662 service; this then developed into a lunch for the elderly and helped a particular group feel much more part of the Christian community.

And how about this example, perhaps surprising, of contemporary use of the BCP?

> At St Simon Zelotes, London, the parish priest Rob Gillion uses the 1662 *Book of Common Prayer* regularly. Faced with the question of how this language could speak, the church has developed an approach of making the language live. 'In the same way that actors work hard to make the language of Shakespeare accessible and alive, so as a church we approach 1662 in the same way. Once a month the All-Age Worship uses the shape and language of BCP Holy Communion, but all ages are encouraged to take different parts of the service. *The Book of Common Prayer* began because of a desire to speak to the common man. We want to create an atmosphere through which people can be touched by God.'

Done well, with an appropriate homily, creativity, and due care and attention given to the words and to the sense of community, this great resource book of our culture can still live and be genuinely life enhancing.

Cross-over jazz

In the early 1990s a CD was produced featuring the vocal group the Hilliard Ensemble and the saxophonist Jan Garbarek. The Hilliard Ensemble is famous for early traditional and contemporary choral music. Garbarek was a jazz saxophonist and improviser. Their CD *Officium* was definitive in the development of what is now called 'cross-over' in music – an organic blend of the traditional and the new which uses the traditional in different contexts or venues to make the old live today.

In the Church we face the '60/40 split'. Recent research tells us that at least 60 per cent of the population finds it difficult to connect with the Church as it is.[24] And there is real evidence that 40 per cent of the population can still find the routines of our church life helpful and meaningful.

This helps us see the clear truth that traditional church is going to struggle to relate to where the majority of people are. But perhaps it can also deceive us into thinking that the traditions of our faith will never be, can never be, a resource in the mission of God to over half the nation. The authors of this book don't see it that way. Indeed, we are saying that if churches look at their worship provision in the light of our missionary values and refocus their worshipping lives, then many of the 'unchurched' would and could find a place where they can encounter God in traditional worship which still speaks to their 'emerging' lives.

Relationship between performer and audience

It's a commonplace of our culture that postmodern people don't like to be preached at, or indeed spoken to, for more than a few seconds on end. But the same people who say that will pay real money to hear Jack Dee, Billy Connolly or Eddie Izzard talk to them all night.

In 2005, Channel 4 filmed the programme *Priest Idol*. The programme charted the sometimes rocky course of a 'green' incumbent faced with a small parish which in the language of education would have been viewed as in 'special measures'. For the Church as a whole there was much to learn from the programme, as will be highlighted elsewhere in this book. The programme particularly drew attention to the cultural gap between church and community. One of the many challenges therefore was how the liturgy of the Church could build fresh connections with a community from which it had become completely estranged. In one of the most compelling parts of the programme the church enlisted the services of a local stand-up comedian to teach the priest how to communicate. He was helpful in two ways. First, he knew the local mindset of the people the church was trying to reach. He had learnt – certainly the hard way – how to make those links. Secondly, he used that knowledge to help the presentation and communication skills of the parish priest. The priest's content was not in question; the way it was presented and communicated was. And his goodwill and readiness to see a church that could speak the people's language was absolutely evident.

At its heart, mission-shaped worship is not so much a matter of new words or new forms and structures as a matter of communicating a common humanity in the presence of a holy God who himself became flesh. And a church whose values for worship include the relational and transformational will constantly seek to do this through the quality of relationships expressed in worship.

Conclusion

We end where we began: worship is the primary calling of all Christians. Every parish church works out that calling by offering something that is rich, diverse and creative. It brings together the liturgical resources of the past and the human resources of the present. A church whose worship is genuinely human and genuinely focused on God will be a missionary church that is transformational, makes disciples, and is in relation to God and others because it has put God first in everything. This is because worship is designed to connect – it is missional. In an age that craves the sacred and is exploring the sacred with open and enquiring fascination, each parish church has plenty to offer.

> The love of God, unutterable and perfect, flows into a pure soul the way that light rushes into a transparent object. The more love that it finds; the more it gives itself; so that, as we grow clear and open, the more complete the joy of loving is. And the more souls who resonate together, the greater the intensity of their love, for, mirror-like, each soul reflects the others.[25]

4 The chores of grace?[1]
Paul Bayes and Tim Sledge

In this chapter we suggest that the work of the Church around the occasional offices can hold its proper place as a core element of a parish mission strategy in the mixed-economy church. The first section will try to tease out our reasons for saying this, and then section 2 will get practical about what it might mean where you are.

1. Some background ideas (Paul Bayes)

The shadow of Christendom

> For it is easy to miss him at the turn of a civilization.[2]

Living in a season of cultural transition is messy and awkward. It can feel very interesting – in the sense of the Chinese curse 'May you live in interesting times'. The constant temptation is to simplify the mess, and church-focused mission risks doing this in one of two ways. Some are saying that the old world of Christendom has already passed away and that the parish church must be wholly and radically different, as of now. Others argue that Christendom will never die, and that all the parish church needs to do is hold its nerve and keep the show on the road. Each of these approaches is gloriously simple. And an incidental benefit is that they provide their adherents with other Christians to insult, so that they can feel both right and righteous.

But they are both wrong. Wouldn't it be better to face the complexity of life more honestly? To grasp the opportunities of late Christendom in a clear-sighted realization that they will not be here for much longer? Because nowhere are those opportunities at the 'turn of a civilization' more evident than in the occasional offices.

In 2003, over 80 per cent of the adult population of the country visited a church building for one reason or another.[3] The majority of those people were attending a baptism, funeral or wedding. If we cannot apply the mission values of the Church to these situations then we are squandering a great gift of God. Of course we cannot expect the nation to flock to church and become disciplined believers because they attended a wonderful wedding or poignant funeral. But there is something profoundly wrong with the holistic vision of a church which relegates these opportunities to 'pastoral care' and then scratches its head about the right way to meet people so that it can 'do mission'.

'Christendom work'

> Today there are numerous signs that the 'Christendom' era in Western culture is fading.[4]

Among these signs are the falling numbers coming to the church with requests for baptisms, weddings and funerals. But Christendom casts a long shadow, and these numbers are still significant in our pastoral and missional scene. For example, we could bemoan the fact that Anglican weddings have dropped by about a half from 109,000 in 1990 to 55,000 in 2002, or that the proportion of church weddings has fallen to just 32 per cent.[5] These figures do not make happy reading, and the trend is obvious. But in the meantime a significant number of couples each year still make the church their first option.

Let's be real. 'Christendom' is certainly passing away. For too long the Church of England in particular has ignored this truth, and has assumed that all is fundamentally well in the Church's mission and that we are just having a bad run of things, a numerical blip. After all, 'people know where we are' and doubtless the church will soon be back to how it was in the 'good old days'.

No. We are called to Christian hope, not facile optimism. On the whole we have not been a healthy or a growing church. But the first of the *Mission-shaped Church* values is to look to God the Holy Trinity, as God is. Our call is neither to ignore the world's trends, nor to simplify them to the point of throwing away the gifts God has given us. The 'mixed economy' (a phrase originally coined by Archbishop Rowan Williams) offers a vision of new and emerging churches alongside a healthy existing church. At present this nuanced and inclusive vision has caught our imagination. And, freshly approached, there is a lasting and vibrant place within this mixed economy for the weddings of the 55,000 couples who come to the Church of England each year with their friends and families – 60 or 70 people on average to each wedding, over three and a half million pastoral contacts in twelve months.

Christendom still has a major influence and we neglect that influence at our peril. And for a parish church 'Christendom work' can bear fruit in discipleship, provided we approach it with as much creativity and energy as we approach fresh expressions of church.

To say this is to court controversy. The phrase 'Christendom work' is drawn from Archdeacon Bob Jackson, who in his influential study *The Road to Growth*[6] reflects on the reasons why the Church in the London Diocese is growing. For him one factor is that London clergy conduct relatively few occasional offices, and so their time is freed up to engage in more proactive evangelistic work and the ongoing nurture of new Christians.

Now the Church needs to take this critique seriously to heart – certainly in the long term. Of course, in one sense London will always be unique; but in another it points the way for the future social shape of the nation. In the meantime, however, as parish churches recognize their new missionary context, one of the best places to start is with what they are already doing and, hopefully, can feel confident and creative about. And for many parishes the issue over occasional offices in the church is not whether it has them – that's a given – it's the way it does them.

We must be honest. For some clergy and local church leaders this aspect of the parish church's work can seem time-consuming, tiring and unproductive – in short, a chore. Nevertheless, in the light of the values of mission, can these offices actually be reframed as chores of grace? Can they regularly be the means by which the love of a sending God can take root in the lives of the significant number of people who pass through our churches at what are key defining points in their lives?

At the heart of *Mission-shaped Church* is the principle of double listening: listening to God and listening to the people and structures that form our context. And every parish church has rich and varied experience of the culture of our nation expressed by those who come for help at these points in their lives. A great deal of work has been done on listening to those who approach the church for ministry through the occasional offices – for instance in the enormously helpful studies by Alan Billings, such as *Secular Lives, Sacred Hearts,*[7] which sees the spirituality of the dechurched in terms of 'cultural Christianity' (close to what used to be called 'folk religion'). But it must frankly be said that the Church has not been good at connecting this work, theologically or practically, with the work of evangelism and of building and growing Christian community.

Our book is trying to make value-connections and to see the practical implications of those connections. In the spirit of listening, then, we will try to come at the occasional offices from the perspective of those who are asking for them. The concept of 'implicit religion' has real value here. As every parish church knows, many people genuinely want to get married in church or have their child baptized or want a Christian burial service, but they simply cannot say why – they are just sure that church is the place to do it:

> 'I want to book the church to have my baby done.'

In an overwhelmingly dechurched/unchurched culture, it takes real courage to come and speak to the parish church from cold, as it were, especially when people cannot articulate their motivation. Cohabiting couples sitting nervously on the edge of the sofa in the vicar's study, driven by an impulse they cannot explain, wondering whether the axe of judgement will fall, should be honoured and loved by the Church; and they respond to a human welcome with surprise and an open warmth.

Our culture sees an increasing desire and need for rituals and rites of passage to mark significant moments in people's lives – however these may be expressed. Providing these in a secular, humanist or generalized 'spiritual' context is a growth sector, and the local press of every large city will carry adverts from these new specialists. But it's the parish church that remains the first port of call for so many. We are given an unmissable opportunity to be at our best as we mark these rites of passage in ways that are welcoming, inclusive and evangelistic.

Attractional and missional modes

> Couples who come for a baptism don't think they're sharing
> the Church's rite. *They* are the hosts; the Church is generously
> invited by the couple to share *their* ceremony. So we need a
> proper humility in honouring their invitation and responding
> accordingly.[8]

Traditional models of evangelism operate from the attractional mode: the
church is saying 'We're attractive. Come to us'. This is fine when it works.
Creating a culture of invitation is a well-tried and successful model. It is
rooted in the invitational character of Jesus and his disciples. John 1.43-46
has examples of both Jesus' invitation to Philip and Philip's to Nathanael:
'Nazareth! Can anything good come from there?' Nathanael asked. 'Come
and see,' said Philip.

But when we work with people through the occasional offices we operate
in a different mode.[9] It is not the church that is going out and inviting. People
are coming with their requests, however they are expressed: 'I want to book
the church, rent the vicar, borrow a church leader to take a funeral'. These
people see the church as their service provider – in more ways than one.[10]
Even in this time of cultural transition, many outside the worshipping church
family still feel able to come and ask the church for its help at these
moments of enormous significance.

Repentance and the 'closed dechurched'

In a well-known graph, *Mission-shaped Church* sketches the national profile of
church attendance and involvement.[11] The graph depicts churchgoers, the
dechurched and the unchurched. We have already made reference to that
graph's categories of 'open dechurched' and 'unchurched' people. But for the
churches the hardest part of this research to hear is that 'twenty per cent of
the population have attended church at some point in their life but were
damaged or disillusioned, and have no intention of returning'.[12] That is one in
five people. It is in this context among others that *Mission-shaped Church*
calls the church to repentance.[13] And every local church leader knows of
people whose disillusion or damage flows from a bad experience of the
response they received when approaching the church over one of the
occasional offices.

Partly as a result of this, and partly out of their own courtesy or ignorance, there is a feeling among many people that they need to ask permission or be invited to come to anything else which is happening in church. The following is a true quote from a former parishioner of Tim's who is now a regular worshipper:

> 'I came to a baptism at your church the other week. Can I ask is it OK to come to church on another Sunday? Would you mind?'

To oversimplify, people outside the church often ask for help and, frankly, we can begrudge these requests because we feel used. At other times, when we hope people will attend our Sunday services for instance, those people feel they need to ask permission to come. And yet the Church of England in particular has regular passing contact with a significant and growing majority of the population. So every local parish church has plenty of opportunities to change those negative perceptions. How should we grasp these?

2. Some practical suggestions (Tim Sledge)

If I reflect back on my time as the vicar of three very different churches, the majority of those who began their journey of faith in my time there did so almost exclusively as a result of pastoral work surrounding occasional offices. It is possible to renew – not to re-brand or re-flavour – but to renew and completely refocus the way God meets people like that when they first approach us for what could be the most significant journey of their lives.

That is when these 'chores' become activities through which the grace of God shines, and people begin that process of discovery and of encountering the living Christ. But in order for that to happen, I needed to look afresh at how we prepare people for baptism and marriage, how we follow them up, and how we walk with bereaved families before, during and after a funeral.

As we mentioned earlier, the differing degrees of Christian influence in all those who receive pastoral ministry from the Church mean that a variety of strategies and approaches and new perspectives will be needed. What follows is not designed to be prescriptive. I am simply making a few rather obvious practical suggestions in order to provoke imagination as to what our occasional offices might look like when they are shaped by the values of mission.

Baptisms

As I begin my reflections on baptism we want to issue a health warning. Our diverse church takes a diverse approach to this sacrament and the circumstances in which it should be offered. My own theology will be evident from our reflections below. But in this book we're convinced that, whatever the nuances of your theology, it is possible through the everyday practice of the parish church to offer the love of Christ to people creatively and warmly.

> 'It's not on! They come one Sunday and take over the place
> and then we never see them again. Why don't those baptism
> families come back to church?'

A similar comment or variation is heard at most churches a week after (or sometimes during!) a baptism service. Behind this refrain is a core question: Why isn't the church making a lasting connection with those who come to the church and make contact with us? Why aren't these people sticking?

In 1900, 609 out of 1000 children were baptized in the Church of England. By 2000, that number was 211 out of every 1,000. That is 21 per cent – nowhere near as many, but still not a bad pond to fish in!

In attempting to address the question of why so many people seem to treat baptism as some kind of spiritual 'wash and go', many churches have sought to work out what they can do liturgically, tweaking or editing the order of service. While this is often needed, it doesn't go far enough and we need to look beyond the underlying question 'How can we get these new people to fit into our ways of doing things?' and be inspired instead by the incarnational value, which 'seeks to shape itself to the culture in which it finds itself'.

One way of seeing the incarnation is to say that God's mission in Jesus was to shape himself around the humanity he was entering; God's mission shape was human as God sought to live among and save humanity. 'He took upon himself the form of a servant' (Philippians 2.7).

In approaching baptisms, therefore, I tried to adopt an approach which was less about saying, 'This is what happens in the service, this is what the church does to you and for you, and this is what you have to do' and more about asking, 'How can we serve you?' and finding out what a couple feel and think about their child and why they want to have the child baptized. In other words, being slow to speak and quick to listen (never easy for me!).

People come for baptism for a vast number of reasons and those reasons need to be honoured – even if we may feel that some of them are a bit 'left field'. In the minds of everyone in the church should be the sense 'Isn't it wonderful that these people want their child to be part of the same family as us? Thank you, Lord.' More grace on the part of a church family might help in the revelation of the greater grace of God through the sacrament itself. In my own experience, for a number of people simply to pluck up the courage and speak to the church, let alone come to this strange building which has never been part of their life's experience, is a huge step to take, and the parish church's pastoral responsibility is to honour that.

Here is another often repeated comment in baptism preparation:

> 'You mean I have to stand at the front and make these promises? I was fearful enough coming to your house let alone church and standing up at the front. I am not sure if I can do that.'

Or as one parent whispered to me as she came up to the dais at the front of the church: 'God, I'm s**t scared, Father!' I am not sure whether she was praying or crying for help, but it both made me smile and reminded me of just what a huge issue this is for many people.

Perhaps the first thing which should be banished in shaping our pastoral response to baptism families is the summoning to the vicarage or, worse still, the vestry hour (normally held at a time of convenience for the church rather than being more 'client centred'). Where possible, let us at least meet the families on their own territory in their own homes if that is convenient and appropriate.

Why do people come for baptism? Here are some reasons I found:

- Part of what happens in the family – a tradition which is passed down.

- A celebration and 'coming out' party. I am amazed at how many come to a baptism and see the baby for the first time. As Alan Billings writes in his excellent and thought-provoking book, *Secular Lives, Sacred Hearts*, it's an unveiling – an epiphany.[14]

- An affirmation of parenthood – rite of passage for the parents.

- A protective feeling of a need for a 'moral world view' for their child.

- A response to wonder – the surprise at a birth and the miracle of it and wanting to do so something but not knowing quite what to do. Interestingly, for this parents could go anywhere, and yet the first port of call for so many is still to turn to the church.

Whatever the reasons, baptism is an amazing missionary opportunity. Family, celebration, affirmation, symbolizing the mysterious and wonderful – these are the things that the traditional parish church does best! These are the very reasons why people are coming. The opportunities are boundless.

story
story
story
story

Some children are baptized in robes or a gown which has lasted four or five generations. Some churches use this both as an opportunity to celebrate the family lineage and also as an evangelistic opportunity to talk about the unbroken strand of God's faithfulness. It is also used as an opportunity for story-telling and for testimony about the importance of baptism.

For example, one church used to ask a member of the congregation to bring their own baptism gown and to share the difference that their faith had made to them and how it started at the point of baptism.

More statistics to encourage

If around 20 per cent of babies are still being baptized in the church, this maps out in my own Diocese of Peterborough to 1,800 baptisms each year. If just 5 per cent of those families began a journey of discovery founded on the promises they had made, then that would be 90 new babies, plus at least their mother and possibly some others – as many as 200 new people – embarking on a journey of faith. An opportunity worth grasping!

Not just a service

The occasional offices are more than just liturgical events. Baptism is more than just a Sunday service. More than any words, the act of worship and its follow-up can show that the church is interested and has something to say about bringing up children.

> 'I have found myself wanting to pray for the baby, but not knowing what to say'.

At its heart, baptism can be seen as a sacrament of relationship. It points to the relationship between the child and God, between the child and the Church and between parents and God. Every baptism is an opportunity for the Church to change shape to accommodate new birth. A new person is added to the Christian family. We welcome that change despite the upheaval. A church which has 'mission-shaped baptisms' is one which has the same outlook. It is willing to have its shape changed because of the new arrival into the family of the Church. This approach does and should put a nail firmly in the coffin of baptisms outside the normal pattern of church worship (with examples such as that in Poole as the exception – see below. How can you possibly welcome anyone into the family of the Church when the Church is absent? Notwithstanding the grace of God, it does seem to render the theology of baptism null and void!

Mirroring the generosity of God's grace

story
story
story
story

One local church set aside a budget for baptism families. At the Thanksgiving they bought a book for the parents and a child's tiny book of prayers for the child. Symbols and gestures such as this are now much more explicit and a vital part of the new *Common Worship* Christian Initiation rites.

At baptism, they didn't scrimp and save on the candles, but (possibly because they can be bought so cheaply nowadays) gave candles to all the godparents and encouraged them to bring the light of Christ into the lives of their godchild. In addition, they thought one step further, investing in a little candle stand. Those preparing the children and their families for baptism then suggested lighting the candle each night when the child went to bed and saying a prayer for them.

There are different approaches to encouraging this practice of parents saying prayers: one example is providing a small laminated card with a couple of simple prayers on it; another is to ask the parents, 'Well, what would you want to pray for? What do you want to say thank you for, and what do you want to ask for?' Their answers are then made up into prayers and presented to the family.

story
story
story
story

Faced with the issue of about 50 baptisms a year, St Aldhelm's, Poole, moved their main Sunday Eucharist to the evening once a month, and gave over the morning to a baptism with a mission intent. A great deal of work was put into the liturgy, the font and paschal candle became the most important furniture in the church, chairs were turned to face each other so that the journey of faith motif could be followed.

> Welcomers who had met the baptism families before sat with
> them in church. The then vicar, Canon Stephen Lake, reflects,
> 'This Baptism Sunday, as it became called, was proving to be a
> mission-shaped opportunity and families went away feeling as
> if they had joined something and with a strong sense that
> God had touched them while they were surrounded by the
> church who had gathered for that purpose alone.'

Here, baptism families in the church often knew each other from ante-natal
classes, and there was an opportunity to develop an initiation rite which felt
both personal to the families and a corporate experience through the
involvement of the church in the hospitality.

The service is only part of the process

In *Finding Faith Today*, John Finney's research back at the start of the Decade
of Evangelism[15] revealed that the average time from initial contact to making
a commitment to Christ was between four and five years. It is arguable that
in the past decade that average time has grown longer. The initial contact
people have with the church may well be baptism. Therefore, mission-shaped
baptisms which are committed to making disciples need to develop a long
game plan. It is encouraging to hear that the service model in Poole was not
a short-term solution to the problem of too many baptisms, but is still going
now as a long-term part of initiation into the Christian community.

In Luddenden, Halifax, the Baptism Visitor –
herself a childminder with two teenagers of her
own – visited all families to prepare them for
thanksgiving and baptism. Across two or three sessions, she
would tell her own story, listen to the story of the families and
then explain what happened in the baptism service, using the
visual symbols of water, oil and light. During the service, she
would take an active part in shaping the liturgy.

She would also follow up with the baptism certificate (home
made) during the week to find out how they had got on,

what they had made of the service and whether they had any questions. This was a crucial part of testing the 'spiritual temperature' of the family.

Perhaps the most significant spin-off from this, and an example of the mixed economy with inherited and fresh expression working in tandem, was the development of a new mid-week congregation – specifically for under-fives.

Toddler Church[16] developed not from a Parent and Toddler Group, but from baptism follow-up, listening to the needs and addressing the question: If these small children are now part of the family of the church, what space are we going to create to allow their new faith and the questions of parents and carers to be addressed? It was felt that there was too great a leap from occasionally attending services and then coming to one baptism to being a regular part of the church. So a series of stepping stones were created. Rather than guess what people wanted, the church spent time asking the families about their needs and the best environment and time for them. This was basic market research based on a simple principle of evangelism: listen first, act second!

The result of this was a church service that was at a suitable time, and a suitable length with content appropriate to this significant group who were looking for a place or home within the church family. As time went on, it became clear that rather than being a stepping stone into 'proper' church, this was church in itself.

Baptism may start for many people as having their baby 'done', but honouring that as a base camp and shaping what we do can and does offer an opportunity for people to begin a journey of belonging and believing and coming to faith in Christ.

Weddings

As Paul cited earlier in this chapter, the number of weddings in church has fallen dramatically, but is still significant. The pastoral and missional reality is that many people of little or no explicit faith still want to get married in church.

The number of church weddings as a percentage of all is similar to baptisms – 22 per cent in 2001. But the post-Christendom truth is that church weddings have been swamped by the number of civil weddings, which now make up 64 per cent of all weddings.

There are a number of obvious reasons for this rise of secular ceremonies, and the Marriage Act of 1994 opened up huge variety and possibilities for marriage venues and the content of the ceremony. However, it's interesting how much recent discussion has arisen over the tension of not being allowed any religious overtones or content in a civil ceremony. Couples who opt for a civil ceremony frequently request a spiritual part to the ceremony 'because of the seriousness' of the decision that they are making. Many also decide for a blessing in a church after a civil ceremony if the church has been unwilling to marry them because one or both parties is divorced.

So, to paraphrase Alistair McGrath's comment on the attractiveness of the gospel, 'We don't need to make Christian marriage attractive. It already is. We need to communicate it in an attractive way.'

In the Lincoln Diocese, the bishop has written the preface to a wedding magazine. It is a good article which sets the tone well and reminds people of the Christian 'option'. Sadly, there are no other Christian articles in the magazine, or any church which presents what they can offer in terms of what a church wedding might be like or how the church can prepare people well for married life together.

St Dionysius, Market Harborough, has a significant number of weddings each year, and many of the receptions are held in the main hotel opposite the church. As a deanery initiative, one of the local curates, together with the Diocesan Evangelist, decided to take a stall at a wedding fair at the hotel. They handed out information about Christian weddings and provided suggestions to families for hymns and readings and many of the 'how tos' of church weddings. Other exhibitors were initially bemused, but delighted to see the church involved. Notable was the number of mothers of the bride who took a particular interest in what the church was offering. The organizer of the event was keen that the church should take part in subsequent wedding fairs and was delighted to discount the exhibitor's fee for the church only!

The preparation

Churches of all traditions which offer marriage preparation have seen it bear fruit.

> story
> story
> story
> story
>
> St Peter and Paul, Moulton near Northampton, runs a programme of work with couples in both preparation and follow-up. They produce a wedding booklet with all the details of planning, choosing hymns and readings etc. They run a marriage preparation morning which they have produced themselves. As part of the follow-up, they also run a 'Developing better marriages' course which concludes with a celebration of marriage and renewal of vows – whether the 30–40 couples at the final service of dedication have been married for 6 months or 60 years. They refer to the process as 'pre-evangelism'. For them the primary message is to show that the church cares about relationships and developing contacts which, without this ministry, would be rather short-term.

This story is one simple and obvious illustration of a church which from the outset seeks to treat an engaged couple and their families not just in a functional way, but as people who deserve to be shown the values of a mission church which is always seeking to shape itself to the needs of the people and respond lovingly and graciously.

All this can be easily done, but for some churches it demands an attitudinal change based on valuing the relational. This change may well take some time, but relationships and friendships are often formed between people within the church and engaged and newly married couples. Because mission takes the long view with God, we too must be willing to play a long game as soul friends to couples and families.

The service

For those outside the church, the church wedding is the main focal point. The big day demands a big service – whatever it may look like!

Values are formed by desire. Mission values are formed from God's desire. They make connections with our basic human desire for love, acceptance, relationship and affirmation; for the couple and their families, as much care and pastoral attention as possible must be paid.

So a wedding service should endeavour to make connections based on these human needs and desires. When it does, those who have simply come for a knees-up can be surprised by God. Surprising numbers of people at weddings say that they use the service as a time for appraisal and reflection on their own marriages or relationships. There are many stories from weddings of long-standing couples who, as guests, have quietly and beautifully recommitted themselves to each other.

The Anglican wedding liturgies provide a significant opportunity to express this love in a way which makes connections with people's lives, and to model the love we celebrate in every aspect of the care provided for families and guests.

Some practical ways of making the liturgy live so that all are active participants rather than witnesses of a legal ceremony:

- Inviting guests before the declaration and vows to make them for themselves as well as for the couple.

- Recognizing the 'leaving and cleaving' by involving the family of the bride and groom in the liturgy and the prayers.

- Speaking openly and boldly about the nature of God's love.

- Offering Christian 'wisdom-values'. In other words, explicitly recognizing the complexity and difficulty of married life and faithfulness, reminding the families that the Christian Church has a long experience of human brokenness and has wisdom to offer about the glory that God can draw from that brokenness. This approach can break the stereotype in people's minds that the Church is a bunch of naive and foolish dreamers who 'always look on the bright side of life', and can lay a foundation for pastoral care in the future, not only with the couple themselves but with their guests.

The follow-up

A number of churches are increasingly developing follow-up plans and ideas to maintain a connection with couples long after the wedding day.

story
story
story
story

In Flore, Northampton, the church put on a celebration of marriage as part of a parish mission. A large number of couples who had been married in the church over the past 30 or so years were invited back, together with all the couples in the small parish. There was a photographer who took pictures of all the couples and by the end of the service had scanned them onto a certificate. There were stories from people about their wedding and the bishop and his wife spoke about the values of Christian marriage. The whole thing was followed by a mini reception where each couple was presented with a pack of information about the Christian faith and their certificate hot off the press! While this did not draw new people to the church it certainly realigned a large number of couples in their marriage and provided a good opportunity to advocate the distinctive nature of Christian marriage.

In a number of churches, annual or regular Valentine's Day services offer an opportunity for a renewal of wedding vows, celebration of love and marriage with opportunities for reconciliation and healing.

story
story
story
story

When St Valentine's Day recently fell on a Sunday, St Matthew's invited back all those who had been married over a number of years. They invited the local church to create a display of the history of weddings in the community. At the end of a positive service of celebration of love and marriage and a reaffirmation of marriage vows, the service leader had invited some Christian listeners from a neighbouring parish to stay behind and pray for individuals and couples and families.

Funerals

More people enter a church building for a funeral than for any other single reason. How then can our funerals be shaped by mission values and what will this mean for the ministry of the Church?

I do not subscribe to the notion that a funeral is an opportunity to preach an overtly evangelistic address and is a real opportunity for people's lives to be changed. I frankly think that this is often an abuse of our position of trust. The funeral service is primarily a pastoral rite but when seen as part of a process of nurturing and healing, it can also be a significant way of helping people to come to a living faith. Therefore our funerals and the surrounding work with the bereaved are a precious and key part of a mission-oriented parish strategy.

The service

How can we make the funeral service connect more with people's lives? For a parish priest it is hard to maintain a freshness if this is the sixth funeral of the week; and yet, of course, for the family it is most likely the first one for many months or years and therefore demands the best that the church can possibly offer, both in terms of content and also in terms of spirit and attitude. *Common Worship* has, I believe, helped this process in many ways. Its liturgy offers a clear opportunity for a funeral both to celebrate a life and to provide some clear pastoral teaching on death and resurrection. Speaking to a society that values the symbolic and non-verbal, there are opportunities for symbols to be placed around a coffin, and more opportunity for sharing and expressing feelings and emotions. The fact is that no matter how new and fresh many of the words of the liturgies are, they are still too wordy for the unchurched; and anyone who is grieving has even less time for words than usual. Therefore, symbols such as treasured personal items (paintings, photographs, golf clubs, ballet shoes, a favourite hat and so on) and movement, and opportunities for expression speak more loudly than the words ever could.

Furthermore, funerals can be transformational. In many communities, particularly rural and more tight-knit communities that still operate on a neighbourhood rather than a network model, a funeral is a community event. Often whole villages gather. If a missionary church seeks to transform the community it serves, then at these key times it can be salt and light – a focus for healing and sharing.

 Tim Alban Jones, formerly of Soham in the Diocese of Ely, reflected in *The Guardian* newspaper on his response to community tragedy – the murder of two young girls:

'The church of St Andrew, in the heart of the community, provided a physical and spiritual focus for the townspeople and visitors. Churches are an appropriate space at a time of crisis. The buildings belong to the communities they serve and, at times of tragedy, it is fitting that they are opened for prayer and reflection.

In the case of St Andrew's, I am aware that its stones have stood for centuries as mute witnesses to countless lesser and greater tragedies that this community has known. The historical presence of bricks and mortar helped to provide a suitable atmosphere of calm and quiet. But it is not the age of the buildings that makes them so apt, it is the fact that they are places of worship; places set aside to encounter God … We are trying to minister and help because of our beliefs; our faith informs our actions. But I do not think that we need to be too explicit about our motives … The fact that Christian women and men are prepared to travel with the broken and bereaved can be a source of comfort to them; and it can help direct them beyond us to God, the ultimate source of comfort, help and hope.'[17]

All Souls and Remembrance Services

Recently, many funeral directors have shown the way to the Church. They have taken our idea of All Souls and made it their own. All over the country, funeral directors take over a crematorium once a month for a memorial service. These are hugely popular and are now part of the package provided by undertakers. Parish churches also have resources to meet this need.

For many churches, the traditional All Souls' Day service to remember those who have died has grown significantly over recent years. Here the local church is providing something to help make sense of shared grief within a community. But while a once a year service is helpful for many, there is also an increasing need for additional rites and pastoral help to assist people in coming to terms with loss and what happens next to them and their loved ones.[18]

 In All Saints, Paston, Peterborough, licensed pastoral workers have set up a bereavement group which meets socially and to share stories. Rather than getting round to everyone to follow up, they are invited to a group with a common purpose. Attendees have found it helpful and comforting and there are opportunities to share a Christian understanding of death. Nearly all the members have spoken of the value of shared relationships.

Services such as this provide opportunities for continuing the journey with those who have been bereaved. They offer a blend of pastoral care and worship but also provide further opportunities to share through stories of the hope which the Christian faith offers. There is more scope here for creative thinking and development of worship and groups for the bereaved.[19]

The great guilt-trip: funeral follow-up

'The one thing I feel really guilty about is that I just haven't had time to follow up the families of all the funerals I have done.'

It's the great guilt-trip – no time to follow up on pastoral offices. A church that seeks to build on values of being incarnational and relational will be aspirational and will also look at ways in which its care and support for families can be ongoing. But by whom and how?

Many dioceses now have Adult Education programmes to train pastoral assistants and ministers. These can be used to great effect not only in supporting the ministry of the priest but also in complementing and strengthening the mission work of the Church.

If our pastoral work is going to be relational, much of that relationship will come from shared experience, and group work building community around this can be fruitful. There are numerous stories of lives transformed through tragedy. At these times, the community of the church comes into its own.

This echoes the importance of prophetic community and friendship outlined in Chapter 6. Follow-up is important across the board. The success and growth of National Childbirth Trust classes has resulted in a number of new mothers carrying on meeting after birth because of the experiences they shared in the run up to the birth of their child. These and other groups embody both mission values and the shared experience of all those who attend. They are relational but particularly incarnational, since they bring together those who might feel isolated through the experiences that they are going though.

Conclusion

One of the problems of the life of a church and priest is that through regularity and pressures of time, the occasional offices and other pastoral work end up defaulting to a process and not an event, and into a programme of things to do rather than being focused on the person.

Is it too fanciful to aim to treat every person who comes to the church requesting occasional offices as a unique person, couple or family and provide something tailor-made for them? Is it too fanciful to see this as a defining point in their lives through which we as the church have the honour of taking people and, in that process, opening up to them the grace of God in baptism, married life or eternal life? The cards are in our hands; and we have an excellent hand to play!

5 Mission-shaped Isle of Dogs
Martin Seeley

As local parishes listen to their communities, the answers can surprise us. For me and for the people of the Isle of Dogs in East London, the mission call was to be rooted in the liturgy of a eucharistic church, and at the same time to develop transforming community ministry that grew out of the pattern of the Eucharist.

The Isle of Dogs is in a context of rapid social change. The population has doubled to nearly 25,000 in two decades. The Canary Wharf development has brought massive change in the built environment. Yet, paradoxically, we find we come to worship not for refuge but to open ourselves to yet more change – the change that God would work in us. As *Mission-shaped Church* declares, 'a missionary church is focused on God the Trinity', with worship at its heart.

Mission-shaped Church goes on to assert the importance of incarnation, lived out by responding to a changing context. That is what we can see God has worked in us on the Isle of Dogs. Through the Eucharist we have inhabited the truths of our faith, and out of that have engaged in building community, which we can see now is our particular gift and charism for the whole parish.

Of course, to be open to God, to subject ourselves to what God is doing with us in our praying and through our lives in this changing culture – all that is hard to accept. We want to figure it out, sort it out, for ourselves. I was bewildered the first several years I was in the Isle of Dogs, trying to understand what God was up to. I could see what God was doing in individuals' lives, but I could not see what God was up to for a community that seemed to be fragmenting and where a large section was bearing a collective grief. Of course I thought I ought to be able to figure it out – it was, after all, my job to discern God's activity. So I felt a strong sense of 'getting it wrong' for some time, because I could not see what was going on. Here are some threads and themes that have become central to the ministry here:

The traditional can resource God's mission

'Don't change the liturgy – it works!' This was the firm – and wise – advice from a friend who knew the parish. Even before I arrived I sensed she was right; my previous experience of parishes in urban communities faced with disruption and uncertainty told me that the familiarity of the liturgy was one of the anchors in people's lives, and that included my own. Humanize it, certainly. Include the kind of ideas that Tim Sledge talks about in this book, yes indeed. But change the shape and structure for change's sake? Not here.

This is not at all because of a feeling that fresh expressions of church or a new church plant would be wrong in principle. But we did as *Mission-shaped Church* asks. We listened to God and to our context – a context of a community living in the midst of massive change. And as we listened, it seemed right to continue to use the traditional resources of the parish to do God's mission.

Two months before I arrived the parish was in the national news. Breaking the 'cease-fire', an IRA bomb had exploded in the northernmost edge of the parish, killing two people, seriously maiming two, and damaging large numbers of commercial buildings and homes. The news focused on the commercial damage, not on the impact on residents. In fact, hundreds of people had to be relocated and many were traumatized. For these people, and residents across the island, this was a triple victimization: first, the locally resented imposition of commercial development centred on Canary Wharf; second, the IRA bomb attracted by the development; and third, being ignored after the bomb. For the long-time residents, families of dockers and workers in the related industries, this was further evidence of the disintegration of their way of life. The church was both affected and involved by the incident. The explosion happened just a few hundred metres from one of the two churches in the parish, and the clergy house sustained damage. The priest based there was quickly on the scene and involved in the care of the victims, and later conducted a memorial service. He and members of the congregation provided continuing care for many of those affected.

Like most parishes today, ours is culturally complex. Since 1981 a predominantly white and fairly homogenous dockers' community has changed and grown into a population made up of three communities: the locals, incoming middle-class professionals, and an incoming Bangladeshi population. The professional incomers further divide into two groups – first are those, usually older, who came to the island early on, in the very late 1970s and 1980s, moving with a 'pioneering' spirit to an area with poor transport links and high deprivation following the closure of the docks, but willing to become involved. The second group, which has appeared in large numbers more recently, are the younger professionals who really choose to live here for convenience – the transport is dramatically improved – and generally seem to have little investment in being part of this particular community.

Anyway, among all that flux and social complexity, I thought I understood why it was important not to 'change the liturgy'. But I came to realize that the fundamental reason lay not in providing a safe haven, a place of solace, but in the second half of my friend's statement – because 'it works'. Only by looking back over some years in the parish have I come to see what this means. The fact is that we need worship to change us.

How does this shaping happen? The worship in the parish of the Isle of Dogs is almost entirely eucharistic (in our parish we're very happy to use the word 'mass'). Like Charles Lowder's parish described in Chapter 2, our parish stands in the 'East End Catholic' tradition, the tradition of catholic liturgy that somehow embodies and takes up the life of the communities of this part of the East End of London and entwines it with the life of God. It seeks to be both local and universal, part of the ordinariness of our daily lives and part of the holiness of God, casual and formal, relaxed and ritualistic. The shape of the liturgy is more important than the words. People are drawn in and included by the drama and action of the liturgy, and in turn that begins to fashion them individually and corporately. In the language of *Mission-shaped Church*, the mission values of a transformed world living relationally flow out of the focus on God as God is. For us the liturgy is the heart of the Church's mission, and it forms and fashions us for our part in extending that mission.

The celebratory and sacrificial meal which is the mass is the model for our life together. At our parish parties there is always far too much food, though occasionally we have run out of wine – fortunately, the wine merchants can perform miracles! Within this whole, each element of the Eucharist has its own transforming resonance. For example, in a community that had been used to everyone knowing everyone else, the Greeting, among other things, challenges us to extend our greeting in the wider community beyond those we know to include the stranger and newcomer. Or, in a community that thrives on story-telling, not to mention gossip, engaging with the stories of our faith transforms our understanding of our lives and the stories we tell about them. But central to the Eucharist is Jesus' life-giving death. For many on the Isle of Dogs, and in countless other communities, change means loss, so the loss represented in the cross touches their humanity deeply. My sense of the great majority of those who are part of the extended – and extensive – church community here is that they – we – live close to the cross. We are just one side or other of it, or under it, or on it. Loss, grief, injustice, tragedy, in matters small and great, never seem far away. But often nor are joy, hope, excitement. The transformation that the liturgy enables people to connect with is the movement from death to life, from the cross to the resurrection.

Representatives before God

For us the most important evolving change has been, in the first instance, not in the form of our liturgy but in its participants and leadership.

When the parish was homogenous, the congregation was similarly homogenous. There were natural family and friendship links between active members of the congregation and the wider community, so the congregation could really be seen to *represent* the community. Both the worship and the outreach work, which included community social activities and youth and children's work, were participated in and, apart from the clergy, conducted by 'people like us'. The church was seen to exist for the community of which, through its participants, it was an integral part. It was an embodiment of the community held in relationship with God.

But what happens to the church when the community starts to become diverse, and fragmented? When I arrived in 1996 there were a few features of the church community that seemed to be a response to the changes in the population of the Isle of Dogs that had started some 20 years before. There were certainly incomers in the congregation who were professionals, but not 'yuppies'. Some had moved to retire here, others had been drawn by the community and the location. Young professionals were moving into the parish in considerable numbers, but were not represented in the congregation.

The leadership of the church – the PCC – talked about being worn out and about the same people always doing the work. After a while I realized that some – not all – of the key leaders were people who had got themselves in, or been placed in, positions of responsibility in order to prevent things happening, to resist change, to defend against the new and unfamiliar. Involvement in leadership, whether in the PCC or in worship, was restricted to those who were deemed trustworthy, which largely had to do with having been there a long time, and being known as 'one of us'. There was a slight air of antagonism in the place. The interregnum had been long and difficult.

However, our aspirations were clear, even if the actions sometimes belied them. The church needed new people and, as best we could, we needed to be a cross-section of the community because we were there to show and share Christ's love in the community. The problem was how to do that, particularly when you are feeling worn out and a bit defensive.

I don't really know how it happened, except that we were challenged to adapt and engage, not resist and retreat. We were also sent some remarkable new people. But the first step that I remember was prosaic: someone gave us the money to put up new notice boards that actually showed the times of the services! And newcomers started to turn up. One Sunday, after I had been there five months, four 'yuppies' came to the parish mass at Christ Church. Two of them came back and stayed (in fact a few years later they were married). They got involved and worked hard at the ordinary things – washing up, putting the chairs away, sweeping the leaves. They came every week, and that meant that when the next 'yuppie' came through the door they saw someone like them and there was a better chance they would stay too.

Within a fairly short period the congregations were beginning to look representative again, and it was not just because of new young adults. There were as many local people joining as incomers, and as the community became more diverse not just economically and socially but internationally, the congregation came to reflect that too. In fact, it has become increasingly multi-denominational as well, so that we have not just more than 20 languages represented, but more than half a dozen ecclesial traditions, ranging from house church to Orthodox.

This diversity now reflects into and out of the liturgy, ranging from a multilingual rendering of the Acts reading at Pentecost to a style of church where newcomers are recruited quickly to take leadership roles in the liturgy and parish programmes. It has also produced a usually unstated but important practice of making sure that every activity and project has people from the different groups in the congregation taking part. In particular this means attending to the local/incomer representation in leadership roles.

Being representative is all very well and usually great fun, but it is for a purpose, and that purpose is mission. Gathered together from the community, the body is built of its diverse and varied parts, with bridges of friendship being built across cultures and traditions. That in and of itself is a sign of the kingdom, but the kingdom imperative is to live that out in the wider community. For everyone, this concerns their own particular sense of vocation to live out their Christian life. But it is also about how the Church together responds and engages in social mission – as *Mission-shaped Church* says, we are valuing the transformation of the whole world, not just of the Church.

The parish has a long history of community involvement, particularly in working with young people. But how do you respond when the community is changing so rapidly? The parish runs an open youth club three nights a week, a pantry for emergency food supplies, a parent and toddler group, and operates two small charities for the relief of poverty. These programmes had been running for many years – and they still do. But in the difficult changes the community was undergoing, there was a need for further response and engagement. What emerged demonstrated two principles: first, be open to whomever and whatever God sends; and second, the mission is centred on and shaped by the truth of God known in the parish liturgy.

Table fellowship

A few months after I arrived in the parish another newcomer turned up and fairly quickly wanted to become involved and help out. His professional life was at the interface of politics, business and public relations and he wanted to apply one of the tools he used there – round-table problem-solving dinner discussions – to the issues the church faced. He wanted to help the church in his community make a difference, and this was the means he proposed. So there began a remarkable series of nearly 20 dinners, held in the vicarage between 1996 and 2000. He acted as host, with his wife and myself, and as chair of the dinner discussions. He was directive and driven – the discussion had a purpose: to identify some achievable steps, for which people around the table would take responsibility, that would benefit the community. There was no agenda – the guests raised issues that concerned them, and as the discussion proceeded, with everyone taking part, a particular theme would emerge. There was usually a point, towards the end of the main course, when it seemed the meal would produce no results. But then, towards the end, something would happen, someone would make a suggestion, or volunteer to do something, and by the time we went round the table asking each person to say what their next step would be, everyone was making a contribution.

On each occasion we invited ten people to be around the dinner table. No one ever declined an invitation and all seemed genuinely pleased – if a little puzzled – to have been invited. The guests arrived at the vicarage in time for a pre-dinner drink and introductions, and some scene-setting stories that would help them engage with what we were about to do.

There would be a mixture of people. Because I and the other hosts were all 'incomers', there were usually two or three other 'local' members of the congregation who were born and bred on the Isle of Dogs or in the immediate area of this part of East London. We would invite a couple of people who worked on the island in community leadership roles – the head of one of the seven schools in the parish, a ward councillor, a staff member of a community development project, a health worker, the manager of the supermarket. To this group we would then add a couple of 'outsiders' from the Canary Wharf business community, or from national government or national community organizations.

What was going on here, and what were the results? First, because these dinners happened in the vicarage, people saw this as the Church at work. Later on, after I was married and our first child was born, we tried holding the dinners in a different location and they did not work the same way – people did not feel that this was the Church undertaking something, though the same people were involved. Location was crucial, and a location that people, particularly those in the community who may have had nothing to do with the church, found both welcoming and clearly 'church'. The process was crucial too; after a couple of dinners, as I learned to trust the process, I found that I was holding people in an event that had a particular shape, in the same way that the celebrant 'holds' people in the process of the liturgy. I had to learn to trust that if the discussion part way through the evening was frustrating and fruitless, something would nevertheless emerge.

There was a mystery about the process of these dinners which takes us back to the liturgy. Those of us hosting them all realized the eucharistic connections. In fact, we adopted the name 'Table Fellowship' from John Austin Baker's book, *The Faith of a Christian.*¹ The eucharistic shape underlined the understanding that all our mission engagement is rooted in our immersion in the Eucharist and takes on such a shape – it is after all the shape of redemption.

There were a host of small outcomes, people connecting with each other, ideas being exchanged and adopted, but two main programmatic outcomes for the parish. The first was a response to a discussion at an early dinner about youth unemployment on the Isle of Dogs. Despite the substantial and growing increase in the number of jobs that the Canary Wharf development was bringing, youth unemployment remained high. At one dinner the idea of setting up a youth employment project was generated and discussed and, crucially, someone came up with a practical way to start it. It took a while, but we did manage to establish the project with one and then two full-time staff providing one-to-one advice and support for young people trying to enter work or training. The project, thanks to the incredibly dedicated and professional staff, has been hugely effective and the most substantial way in which the church has adapted its social outreach to tackle one of the fundamental problems in the community.

The second main outcome was also eucharistic in shape – another meal. This time it was a response to how to let St Luke's church be better known in its neighbourhood. St Luke's has a small congregation in a nondescript building (a hall with a small chancel added on), in the middle of a housing estate. The idea emerged, during a table fellowship dinner, to host a monthly free Sunday lunch for anyone who wanted to come. One of the participants at the dinner gave some money to cover the cost of food for a few months, and so it started. The lunches were hard work but effective, and became known in the local neighbourhood, particularly when people realized that 'free' really meant 'free'. Significantly, the lunches attracted involvement from the Bangladeshi community too, so the gathering each Sunday became a very inclusive and representative group.

So for us, mission that makes a difference in the community is rooted in the liturgy and is about making and deepening relationships, often, it seems, around a meal. For the Church to be really engaged in responding to the challenges of the gospel in a particular place, a great deal of relationship building – networking – has to happen. We cannot assume that the Church has a role, just as we cannot assume that people know what the Church is about. So essential to the engagement is being involved, getting known, making relationships. It is making 'establishment' mean something at the local level. With that goes a mind-set, an attitude that the Church does have a mission in the community and is called to be engaged, and in turn that means being open to whatever the call might be.

What surprised me, then, was that this process of engagement, through Table Fellowship and a range of other networking exercises, also had an impact on the congregation. There was almost a circle here – mission rooted in liturgy, engaging in the community, which in turn changes the congregation. What I noticed was that people involved in community issues in the parish started coming to church. One area of growth in the congregation then became new people who were working in the community on the issues we had shown we cared about.

And all that feels like Isle-of-Dogs-shaped, mission-shaped Church to me!

6 Friendship, community and mission
Paul Bayes

This chapter looks at the 'friendly parish church' through the lens of mission.

> The creation of living, breathing, loving communities of faith at
> the local church level is the foundation of all our answers.
> Proclamation of the gospel, charismatic gifts, social action and
> prophetic witness alone do not finally offer any real threat to
> the world as it is ... when set apart from a community.
>
> It is the ongoing life of the community of faith that issues a
> basic challenge to the world as it is, and offers a visible and
> concrete alternative.
>
> The church must be called ... to rebuild the kind of
> community that gives substance to the claims of faith.[1]

Despite all the recent stress on 'friendship evangelism', this chapter argues
that the Church hasn't fully grasped the extraordinary gift God gives his
children when he gives them one another. Simple Christian friendship is
more subversive, more mission-focused and more prophetic than the
Church has realized.

Over the last 20 years, lots of excellent resources have become available to
help churches improve the quality of their welcome or their common life, or
to build up their small group structure.[2] Any sensible PCC will be using them
and constantly working to improve its relational life. But becoming a warm,
friendly and open community is not a functional gimmick to drag in some
new punters. It is an outworking of the Christian gospel, and like every other
gospel thing it will be marked with the love, the suffering, and the
overcoming truth of Jesus Christ.

A missionary church is relational

It is characterized by welcome and hospitality. Its ethos and style are open to change when new members join.[3]

The friendship factor

Many Christians and many parish churches are suspicious of the word 'evangelism'. It comes to them with too many unpalatable overtones and implications. But almost everyone agrees in principle that community and 'fellowship' are necessary to any church. Our understanding of pastoral care, nurture and discipleship is built on the assumption that Christians will be relating to one another, week by week, when they meet.

Building on a good deal of research and theological reflection, *Mission-shaped Church* points to the reality of a neighbourhood/network world. It brings lots of evidence to bear and makes its case convincingly. But this is an uncomfortable reality for many in the parish church. At first sight it seems to undermine the value of the local, the rooted, the human, and to replace them with a shuttling, loud, electronic, cold, loveless world that only the affluent can access.

In such a context church people have a choice. They can go into denial, become grumpy old men and women, huddle together against a world they dislike. Or they can see the opportunity they have, precisely because of their rootedness, to bring a challenge and a message to some parts of this changing context. In the 1990s Robert Warren wrote about missionary congregations and developed this well-known snapshot of church life (see p. 80):

In the years since, of these three aspects of the missionary congregation, community – one of honest and supportive friendship – has emerged as more and more important, specifically at the point of overlap with mission.

Now it seems pretty obvious to say that this emphasis on 'friendship evangelism' can only be built on a commitment to friendship. Those who reflect on the health and growth of the Church come back over and over again to the importance of what Professor David Ford calls 'the community of the face'.[4]

This commitment of the Church to authentic relationship is something that is recognized by the wider world. Our society expects friendliness from Christians, and it minds if it doesn't get it. In late 2005 the secular media were tickled by a *Church Times* report unpacking and listing examples of rudeness in churches – the disabled woman hauled to her feet by a sidesperson during the national anthem, the wheelchair user who was advised to go home instead of attending a service, the vicar who was told by a churchwarden that new families 'weren't really our type', etc. This story made the headlines because of the mismatch between what society expects of believers and what it sometimes gets.

However, even if churches succeed in being faithful to the relational value, they are not always thanked for it. This is because, normal and everyday as it is, Christian parish community can be profoundly counter-cultural.

Prophetic friendliness

As well as being increasingly network-based, our society is privatized and fragmented. Of course, not everyone sees that as a problem. The self-sufficient and the wealthy in particular tend not to mind it.

When the sharing of the Peace began to be introduced into the Eucharist 30 or more years ago, it quickly became a bone of contention. It was seen as a physical symptom of a church that was looking too hard for friendship. A coalition grew to oppose it. This had various strands. They included emotionally inhibited Englishmen and Englishwomen ('Have we been introduced?') and those whose theology had no room for the human community ('It's just me and my Maker, Vicar!'). There were also many people who were afraid that a cheap togetherness would devalue the mystery, and even the truth, of the faith:

> In a sense, the more shy and retiring we are, the better.
> Nothing is more tiresome than the gregarious young priest
> who overwhelms his parishioners with 'friendship', slaps
> people on the back and asks them to call him 'Tom'.[5]

Indeed, that gregarious young priest became a stock comedy character, and has remained one for over 30 years. He took over this comic role from Alan Bennett's clergyman, who, goodness knows, is still recognizable enough:

> Some of us think life's a bit like that, don't we? But it isn't. Life,
> you know, is rather like opening a tin of sardines. We all of us
> are looking for the key. And I wonder how many of you here
> tonight have wasted years of your lives looking behind the
> kitchen dressers of this life for that key. I know I have.[6]

If you laugh at this it is because you know that Bennett's pompous ass is living in a world of his own. But what is funny about 'Tom' seems to be that he wants to live in our world – to be friendly. According to his amused or angry critics, poor 'Tom' has missed the point. Doesn't he know (they say) that it is precisely aloneness, or aloofness, or mystery that draws his parishioners to church in the first place?

Even preferment doesn't get 'Tom' off the hook. Monica Furlong grumbled about:

> a habit of speaking about a bishop in conversation by his title
> and Christian name – Bishop Tom, Bishop Jim, Bishop Timothy
> . . . I fear what it indicates is a willed intimacy, a pretence that
> bishop, clergy and laity are on much closer terms than they
> actually are. It is not very convincing.[7]

Although the quotes above were written by Christians, most of those who laugh at 'Tom' or 'Bishop Tom' would not see themselves as members of the community of faith. If they do ever go to their parish church it is not for friendship. They find that elsewhere, if they seek it at all.

So the Anglican parish church has become a source of mockery for today's 'cultured despisers of religion' precisely at the point of friendship and community. Their toes still curl at the very thought of sharing the Peace, being friendly, smiling. In the eyes of the chattering world these things are right up there with strumming guitars, waving tambourines and the Alpha course, as sharp indicators that the Church has lost its way.

With unusual fortitude and consistency, in the teeth of all this opposition from the socially comfortable (or from those so deeply wounded that they no longer feel their loneliness), many of the parish churches of England have chosen to be friendly. They have invested their lives in the relational value. And paradoxically this has been a most unpopular choice.

Nothing in the last half-century – not the ordination of women, not *Faith in the City*, not even *Common Worship* – *nothing* has proved as annoying as the Church's commitment to friendliness. It is the antithesis of contemporary 'cool'. I heard echoes of it every time I asked in our church who had had a birthday and every time we sang 'happy birthday' to them (it happened about four weeks out of five).

Against all this mockery there stands the local parish church. Typically, it is unique in its wider community. It will contain disproportionate numbers of the lonely, the elderly poor ('When someone shakes my hand at church, it's the only time in the week anyone touches me'), single parents, younger children, those with a learning disability, and those who choose community not because it is cosy or an escape, but because Jesus promised that he would be found there.

> Tony arrived at the church and 'found a lovely group of people – I felt as if I had come home. Now I have something to offer back.'

The friendliness of the local church is a prophetic mission act, valued most by those who need it most. Like all prophecy, the friendliness of the Church confronts. It demands a decision, and large numbers of people decide for it.

So to make this talk about 'prophetic friendliness' real will be to grow the Church, but it is not a church growth technique. For a stranger to describe a community as friendly means that friendship has been offered, and offered openly, without ulterior motive. And when it is openly offered, somewhere in the heart of the stranger Christian friendship is recognized for what it is – an agent of the mission of God. It is not normally refused.

Open friendship

> The son of man has come eating and drinking, and you say,
> Look, a human being, a glutton, a drunk, a friend of taxmen
> and sinners. (Luke 7.34)

Winston Churchill liked pigs. When asked why, he replied, 'Cats look down on you as your superiors. Dogs look up to you like your servants. But a pig will treat you as an equal.' The German theologian Jürgen Moltmann would have seen Churchill's point: 'One does not have to submit to a friend. One neither looks up to nor down at a friend. One can look a friend in the face.'[8] He goes on to say this:

> The closed circle of friendship among peers is broken in
> principle by Christ . . . For this reason Christian friendship also
> cannot be lived within a closed circle of the faithful and the
> pious, of peers in other words, but only in open affection and
> public respect of others.[9]

Moltmann coined the phrase 'open friendship' to describe this way of relating. You see it every week across the Church.

story
story
story
story

Joanne was invited by a workmate to an *Alpha* course. In the traditional *Alpha* way, the evenings began with a meal. By the end of the course she had committed her life to Christ and was involved in a small group in her new church. Exactly how had the course helped?

'I came three or four times before I even started listening to the talks the bloke was giving. They were very chatty and cheerful, but I wasn't listening. And I never dared ask any questions in the little groups. I couldn't think of anything to say. No, I just came for the meal. It's not that I was hungry or needed the food or anything, but it was just so nice to talk to people who wanted to talk to me. After a few weeks I thought I'd better start listening to the talks. By then I'd missed half the teaching. But it didn't matter. My new friends told me what I'd missed, over the meal the following week. And they answered my questions down the pub afterwards, not in the little groups. So it all started making sense. And I became a Christian.'

The friendship we are talking about here is not to be faked, and indeed it cannot be faked successfully. Politicians and chat-show hosts attempt to do so all the time, to their own loss. The late Hughie Green, with his wonderfully nervous, insincere smile, referred to everyone as 'friends'. In the TV comedy *The Office* the manipulative boss, David Brent, says, 'I suppose I've created an atmosphere where I'm a friend first and a boss second . . . probably an entertainer third.' We laugh because we know what a fraud he is. But we don't laugh much, or for long. Like Alan Bennett, *The Office* is too true to be funny.

'Friends open up to one another free space for free life.'[10] The very word 'friend' is rooted in older words that mean 'free one'. Shouldn't that freedom be at the heart of what Christian parishes seek to do in building their common life? And can't people tell at once if it's replaced with the sort of welcome that is only a preparation for asking new people to help with the cleaning rota?

story
story
story
story

Ruth has begun going to church again after a long while. She is gradually reconnecting with her faith, but her life is demanding and weekend time is at a premium. She loves her small local church 'because there is no pressure on me. They never nag. They're pleased to see me when I can come.' There is an open response to her commitment. It is negotiated rather than imposed.

If we are indeed one, what is our relationship to be? Friendship. 'The friend is the new person, the true person, the free person, the person who likes to be with other people.'[11] Jürgen Moltmann sketches what a church of open friendship would look like:

> What would it be like if Christian congregations and communities were no longer to regard themselves only as 'the community of saints' or as 'the congregation of the faithful' but as such a 'community of friends'? . . . Then they would have to assemble in grass roots communities that would live close to the people and with the people in the friendship of Jesus.[12]

It could be a fresh expression of church, but it also sounds like a parish to me. The Roman Catholic contemplative Carlo Carretto says the same thing, but he points to the foundations:

> Today's people . . . want a Church made of friendship, of genuine contacts, of mutual interchange of little things. But more than anything else, a Church that feeds them with the Word, a Church that works with them by physically taking them by the hand, a Church whose face is like that of the Church of Luke, of Mark, of John, a Church that is just starting – that smells of beginnings.[13]

'A church that is just starting' . . .? Yes – but again, not only a fresh expression of church. Church wherever it is expressed freshly.

Positive friendliness

'Such a friendly church.' Despite all the grumpiness I mentioned above, when you hear this said inside a church building it is not usually meant as an insult, but a compliment. Open friendliness is an authentic note of mission – and making it truly so is the challenge facing local church leaders, because of course 'a friendly church' is not the same thing as a church full of people who are friends of one another. If you are new, that can be the mark of a most *unfriendly* church, and its symptom is the cluster of backs presented to strangers by church people huddling together over coffee after the service, or the jolly in-jokes in the notices. Nor is friendship the same thing as 'welcome', important as welcome is.

> story
> story
> story
> story
>
> Susie had been coming to church for eighteen months. On her first Sunday she was warmly drawn in by the church's 'welcome team' and on the strength of this she committed herself to the community. She came in tears to the vicar. 'You all made me so welcome on my first day here', she sobbed, 'and yet I don't know anyone any better now than I did then.'

As Robert Warren says, 'Real welcome is what happens after we have said "hello".'[14] This has implications for the small groups in a church, but also for the reality of an open friendship that spills out of rotas and methods and just invites people round for – yes, coffee. Or lunch. Or a natter. Anyone who believes that these things are unconnected to mission has not understood the incarnation.

It is as St Paul might have said, 'My church can organize cells and groups for people and angels, it can train its leaders to postgraduate level, it can explore the deepest issues of faith and life; but if it has no friendship, we are no better off.'

If 'real welcome is what happens after we have said "hello"', then it needs to spill over beyond Sunday church. It is doing so everywhere, and has been for over 40 years, through the growth of what began educationally, as 'courses', and then became places for friends to meet.

The art of course friendship

Churches with no small group system are impoverished, lacking as they do the natural space and context for the development of friendship; almost all parish clergy agree about that, and so do all the gurus of church health and growth. This understanding has grown on the Church in England for over 40 years. In the 1960s the relational value received a boost through Lent courses such as 'People Next Door' and 'No Small Change'. These were often explicitly ecumenical, at a time when discovering other church traditions was a new and daring venture. For many people, including my own parents, they opened the door to a new dimension of Christian discipleship.

The 'No Small Change' group that began in my parents' home in Lent was still going, fortnightly, twelve years later.

My father, a taciturn Yorkshireman, churchwarden of his church but with no understanding of himself as a spiritual leader, discovered what it meant to write and pray his own prayers in the group, and drew closer to God as a result. His story was repeated thousands of times across the Church. The relational and discipleship values were in action, if only for six weeks in the year to start with.

In many places Lent courses and house groups are still going strong. But they have a bad press, because a good deal of research and evidence has shown that they can get stuck in clubbishness and comfort – or, worse, they can be seen as a penance which decent Christians should inflict on themselves in the season of our Lord's suffering. As a result, many of those who want to renew mission values in the church prefer more focused and long-term discipling in cell groups or something of the kind. But we live in a changing culture.

story
story
story
story

Gill is a management consultant living in Petersfield. With her husband Martin she leads 'Ish', a group of a dozen or so members of her parish church who are twenty- or thirty-ish. Like many similar groups, Ish meets in monthly 'terms' for discussion and sharing, looking at the world from a Christian angle, giving its members permission to be honest about their difficulties, confusions and ambiguities, and working to equip and build up the members for their lives as believers in the world. These articulate, committed people have reached levels of honesty and openness that make the group a real resource in their lives. Their home-based church life complements their weekly worship, rounding their lives as Christians in their town and their networks.

So perhaps for Gill, and for people like those in her group, traditional church ways of study, for example a six-week Lent course, are outmoded and would no longer be helpful?

'I disagree completely. The lives of the people here are built around short-term projects. Look at me – I have a portfolio lifestyle, I'm paid to do project work, it's the way I think. A six-week faith project sounds like a really good idea. In fact why isn't the Church learning from it? I would have far more sympathy with a church built in a project-centred way than with one that expects me to do the same thing week in, week out.'

The picture here is one of serial group life – recognizing the importance of intimacy and accountability, but maybe shaking free of the expectation that everything the Church does properly has to be permanent. Perhaps serial small-group life, project-based group life – an Advent course, a Lent course – has more to say in a postmodern world than the Church has imagined.

And so do the small groups we have had for many years.

Natural networks and Ladies' Fellowships

In a neighbourhood/network world the mission of the Church will flourish where natural networks and their friendships are strongest. In many parishes the age groups where this is true are secondary school young people, and the retired and widowed. Ladies' Fellowships, Men's Societies and Mothers' Union branches across the country are rightly valued for their contributions to pastoral and community work; but in a mission-shaped Church they should also be explicitly honoured for their gifting and experience in growing the Church. They often do it by including and offering comfort to those in need, most of them dechurched or unchurched people. For those who have suffered illness or bereavement, finding Christian friends who have walked the same road of suffering leads easily and naturally to a desire to find out more about the faith that sustains those friends. This work of the parish church builds on existing networks and people-groups, and so it will never be enough to touch the whole of a fragmented society. But in a mixed-economy church, the Ladies' Fellowship and the MU can be missionary and evangelistic at their core. As groups their mission is not normally cross-cultural (although as individuals many of the over-60s are at the cutting edge of cross-cultural mission, in an age when the only acceptable place for real intergenerational meeting is in the conversations between grandparents and their grandchildren). But in a parish church, the human networking of the mission of God is wholeheartedly done by, among others, the Ladies' Fellowship.

Ivorne's husband died. Her friend Molly invited her to the monthly Ladies' Fellowship in her church, which always began with a Eucharist led by the vicar. The service, a simple said *Common Worship*, was very strange and new-fangled for Ivorne, who had not been to a 'normal' church service since the 1950s. But the service ended and the tea-urn came out. The vicar vanished. And the warmth of friendship among the Ladies' Fellowship, the informality of their life, and the fact that many had themselves been widowed, all added up to a real attractiveness for Ivorne. In that context even the unfamiliar worship wasn't too unpleasant – and even began to be helpful.

From this Ladies' Fellowship Ivorne joined an *Alpha* course provided by the church, and from there went into a weekly home group. For Ivorne both the *Alpha* course and the regular group were of a piece with the life of the Ladies' Fellowship – courteous, gentle, relational, intimate and real.

John fought as a paratrooper in the Second World War and was a prisoner of the Japanese, losing a leg in the conflict. He was a community gatekeeper, chairing his local British Legion branch and helping run the over-60s club at his local community centre. And churchgoing had been a habit of John's and source of comfort. But when his church ran the Emmaus course, something clicked for John. By then churchwarden of the church – a church which greeted Emmaus with some suspicion – he found his faith coming alive for him in ways which made sense of his community involvement as a Christian ministry rather than a duty. Within the church family he advocated and supported the nurture process as one who had been personally blessed by it. Because his personal credibility was so high, his support for the course opened the eyes of many in the church to see nurture and process evangelism as a normal and integral part of Christian life. None of this was quick or easy, and many in the church still found it difficult to enter fully into the idea that they themselves had a ministry of their own. But John, as a 'man of peace' in the community, led the way. His contribution transformed his community also. His atrocious experiences in the war had not embittered him, and he brought to the local British Legion branch a spirit of openness and forgiveness which was greatly appreciated among others in the town, and caused the branch itself to grow and its influence to increase.

These are real examples. They focus what friendship and community can mean in the service of mission. They both come from a single benefice. They point to tens of thousands of others across the Church. They arise from the traditional, centred strength of Anglicans in England as God has shaped it today. No mixed-economy Church shaped for mission can afford to neglect them. On the contrary it seems to me that the task for parish clergy and lay leaders in every place is to highlight, honour, celebrate and affirm each one of them as essential contributions to the mission of God in that place.

7 On being mission-shaped civic church: the view from Wimborne Minster

John Holbrook

On the face of it, civic churches might seem as far from the world of *Mission-shaped Church* as it's possible to get. But I believe it would be a mistake to think so. For me, and for many of my colleagues involved in civic ministry, the report has encouraged us; but it has also given us a helpful critique.

The civic church

> I believe I'm called to serve the city, the congregation think I'm called to serve them.
>
> (Civic church leader)

In Wimborne we have tried to engage in mission by prioritizing our outward-facing relationships with the wider society. This means that we've had to be very watchful of the quality of our inner community life – civic churches are too often seen as cold and forbidding communities. But in building relationships with civic leaders, our mission opportunities are clear. Even at the last gasp of Christendom, civic society gives its churches a privileged platform from which it can both bless and challenge, and in Wimborne we're trying to make the most of that platform while it lasts.

On New Year's Eve I'm invited to join the Mayor on the balcony of a local hotel, overlooking the square thronged with over a thousand people, and asked to bless the crowd. I am given an open microphone to commend the Christian faith, pray and wish everyone a 'Happy New Year'. This is only one, if the most public, opportunity to arise from the ongoing partnership between the church and our local councils. We lead prayers at council meetings and have built good working relationships with councillors and officers. The annual round of civic services, St George's Day parade, Folk Festival worship, Remembrance Sunday and carol services brings thousands of irregular worshippers into the church. The church helps create community by deliberately behaving as if it exists and helps to create meaning by contributing a major part of the town's shared story.

For us this annual round is not a chore, but a way of developing ongoing relationships. These provide firm ground when public relationships in the town become fractious and need some healing.

> story
> story
> story
> story
> The vicar of one city centre church deliberately stood alongside members of the local council as they endured a bitter planning row. She offered pastoral support and while remaining neutral over the substantive issue, was repeatedly reported declaring that the councillors were 'not fools or knaves or dupes, but elected representatives doing what they believed was best'.

This kind of ministry will go beyond a narrow vision of chaplaincy, blessing whatever happens to be there. Not far from our parish, as a result of the careful building of relationships, Purbeck District Council invited the Rector of Wareham to chair its Ethical Standards Committee. And all over the country civic churches are often the only places where the town has a neutral space, for example to host a Thanksgiving service on the death of a controversial Member of Parliament.

Providing a safe forum for informed debate has proved in recent years to be a good model for churches to serve the wider community and offer a Christian perspective. At the last General Election, in many constituencies churches were the only forum in which candidates were prepared to share a platform and therefore offered some of the few opportunities for real debate. These ecumenically organized gatherings also demonstrated the Church's own ability to live with diversity and mature discussion.

Church as disciple-making community

But how can civic churches live out the disciple-making value of *Mission-shaped Church*? Here is a challenge, as discipleship cannot happen in isolation from community. We have already seen that there are great strengths in the relationships which civic church can form with other partners, but this has its shadow side. Many people choose to attend civic churches because they have a 'privatized spirituality' which they want to express without too much fellowship and camaraderie. This is the opposite to the 'prophetic friendship' that Paul talks about elsewhere in this book. In addition civic churches often attract people from widespread geographical networks rather than one community and include a significant proportion of occasional worshippers.

This isn't just a civic-church issue. All churches share the contemporary tension between the longing for community and the desire for solitude. Indeed, some mission strategies, for example those influenced by the Willow Creek movement, emphasize the value of anonymity and space in the lives of seekers. And this can be fruitful and helpful at the beginning of a journey of faith.

But there is a particular dilemma for mission-shaped civic churches in serving both their inner and outer lives. This balancing act is complicated by the ambivalent expectations of belonging held by some members. *Mission-shaped Church* brings a necessary challenge here. Commitment to the relational value leads me to believe that the expectation of anonymity needs to be questioned, even as we work with it.

In any case my experience is that where civic churches adopt generally recognized good practice, they see numerical and spiritual development. This might be through RCIA (Rite of Christian Initiation for Adults), Alpha and Emmaus groups, a structured catechumenate, regular confirmation preparation or many other programmes.

So in Wimborne the Minster offers short courses, quiet days and lectures, special liturgical opportunities through Lent and Advent, and spirituality events such as a '24/7' vigil when the crypt is kept open for a whole week, day and night, for private prayer. We also deliberately invite a variety of preachers, who speak with a range of voices, as a means of encouraging members to engage in mature discussion on difficult issues. And we have worked alongside Scripture Union in a 'Lifepath' programme, originally devised for Durham Cathedral and Jervaulx Abbey. This is designed to allow historic church buildings to tell their own stories and the story of faith.

A five-day event drew over 600 nine- and ten-year-olds for a varied programme of workshops, drama and worship.[1]

story
story
story
story

As part of our 1300th anniversary celebrations in 2005, we invited every member of the church community to take semi-monastic vows of commitment for one year. Sherborne Abbey later developed this idea by encouraging people to draw up a personal Rule of Life. The Minster, founded as a mission church by Saint Cuthburga, offered an opportunity to take the following seven vows in front of the bishop:

Inspired by the example of St Cuthburga,
I commit myself to live this year as a disciple of Jesus Christ
*   guided by the Holy Spirit, to the glory of God the Father.*

I promise to

- *Pray daily*

- *Read the Bible regularly*

- *Attend public worship faithfully*

- *Commend the Christian faith by word and deed*

- *Fashion my life according to the example of Christ*

- *Give and forgive as generously as God has given to and forgiven me*

- *Promote Christian Unity*

We were astonished when a total of 400 people undertook to live by the vows which provided the themes for a series of sermons and featured in every major act of worship during the celebrations. It was spiritually a most significant moment in the church's life.

Civic churches as transformational

Sometimes it is attitudes, mind-sets and prejudices that need to be challenged. In Wimborne we have tried to play our part in changing minds over some of the most pressing issues of our day.

story
story
story
story

The Minster has promoted trade justice for over 20 years and achieved recognition as a Fair Trade organization. Church members have been thrilled to see the town council applying for Fair Trade status. We have now begun the process of achieving the parallel benchmark for good ecological practice.

Today's civic communities are often multi-cultural and churches may find themselves discovering an important task in challenging prejudice and developing a mature vision for civil society. Birmingham's Anglican cathedral played a vital role in the city's Refugee Council and public debate about asylum-seekers and immigration.

As diverse inclusive communities, civic churches can offer a transformational vision that goes beyond the associational grouping of the like-minded. I believe one of their key contributions to the 'mixed economy' of the mission-shaped Church is that they are themselves mixed communities.

Although ecclesiastically quite traditional, civic churches can act as agents of radical change. If they regard the wellbeing of their towns and cities as a sign of their effectiveness, they commit themselves to improving the world. As such they play their part in God's mission.

Civic churches and letting God be God

> Be always near us when we seek you in this place. Draw us to
> you when we come alone and when we come with others, to
> find comfort and wisdom, to be supported and strengthened,
> to rejoice and to give thanks. Amen.
>
> (Prayer at the rehallowing of Barnes Parish Church)

The best welcome literature in our great historic churches invites the visitor
to look beyond history and architecture and recognize that they are
primarily places of worship and prayer. Alongside many other churches with
large numbers of visitors, we offer prayers over the public address system to
give people an opportunity to share in the daily cycle of worship.

Michael Sadgrove, Dean of Durham, wrote:

> Worship is one of the best tools for evangelism we have.
> Cathedrals invest so heavily in this because there is a
> 'converting' quality to liturgy when words, silence, music, ritual
> actions and architecture combine to create a theatre of the
> soul that speaks of the holiness and love of God.[2]

To what extent does the worship of civic churches reflect the whole nature
of the God who is revealed as Father, Son and Holy Spirit? Our language,
focus and hymnody at large official services will most often stress the
transcendent majesty of the Father or of Christ in glory, though this has
relaxed in recent years. Many of those in senior civic roles have a strong
sense of public service; however, there is a need to be careful of uncritically
using 'throne theology' in the presence of those who sit on (metaphorical)
thrones!

In large churches with small chapels, the intimacy of more private spaces can
offset the grandeur of the public stage. We have also broadened the types of
worship by starting new congregations. However, my overall observation is
that if there is a weakness it is usually in failing to give adequate weight to
the Holy Spirit, who is sometimes domesticated as the inspirer of artistic
creativity and rarely allowed to blow where he will.

In church tourism circles the great aim has been 'to make tourists into
pilgrims'. Examples of good practice include literature, signs, quiet areas

designated for reflection, opportunities to request prayer and, above all, church members to welcome and act as guides.[3]

story
story
story
story

Many churches have been exploring the use of installations to encourage visitors to engage with the building at greater spiritual depth. Prayer trees, candles, post-it boards, water, world maps, stress pebbles, daily newspapers, doodle sheets, bubbles, images of Christ and works of art are just some of the activities we have offered. The largest and most dramatic is the 'Labyrinth', a giant stroll-through prayer walk, with personal stereo guide.[4]

However, visitors are guests and will make their own sense (or non-sense) of what they experience. Churches can only ensure that visitors receive the best and most accurate impression, true to our values and our faith. Despite the busyness of much-visited churches, there is often a holy stillness.

Civic churches are also well placed to make the most of the opportunities that arise from the annual cycle. Worship that resonates with the seasons will resonate with the seasons of people's lives. In our culture this is particularly true of the autumn cycle of remembering: All Souls, All Saints and Remembrance.

story
story
story
story

'Resonance' uses history as an archive in offering styles of worship for postmodern culture. Typically an evening includes acts of worship and zones or stations (e.g. listening, storytelling, anointing, confession and creativity). Cathedrals are chosen as the venue because 'They are places of safety for Christians and non-Christians alike. They are associated with spirituality in a way many other church buildings are not.'[5]

At the Minster we have tried to fulfil the primary *Mission-shaped Church* value by our strong focus upon worship. We aim to reflect the wholeness of

God in the variety of styles and the offering of hospitality. However, through lack of imagination, I don't believe that we always make the most of the opportunities offered by our privileged place in civil society and the resources we enjoy. We're typical of other civic churches up and down the country. Here, as in so many other ways, *Mission-shaped Church* brings us a challenge and an encouragement to do better.

8 The place of nurture within a mission-shaped Church
Tim Sledge

This short section seeks to bring this value to bear on what the local parish church can do to make and grow mission-minded believers, and points to nurture courses as the royal road to relational growth:

> A missionary church is active in calling people to faith in Jesus Christ, and it is equally committed to the development of a consistent Christian lifestyle . . . It encourages the gifting and vocation of all the people of God . . . It is concerned for the transformation of individuals, as well as the transformation of communities.[1]

 Jane was 24 years old. She had been asked to be a godparent for a friend's daughter. She had agreed enthusiastically, but realized that she was not baptized. Keen to make promises for herself and to find out more about the Christian faith, she went to her local church to ask if she could be baptized. The local vicar said 'Sorry, we are not doing any baptisms or preparation this year. Could you come back in about ten months?'

The nurture group: phenomenon and scandal
In the last quarter-century one third of all churches in the country have set up a nurture course of one kind or another. This remarkable trend has grown in response to evangelistic initiatives at which adults were making commitments, but had little or no prior knowledge or experience of Christianity.

Bishop John Finney speaks of his experience in the Wakefield Diocese, saying that many people are four generations away from any Christian knowledge or have anything more than a smattering of received 'folk-lore' as their understanding of the faith.[2] This means that people are much further back in their Christian understanding than the Church thinks.

Generation 1:   Parents and children attend church. All have some knowledge of the faith and of the Church.

Generation 2:   The children, now grown up, do not go to church, but send their children to church. All still have some knowledge of the faith; for some it is fresh in their minds, for others it's part of the 'history of childhood'.

Generation 3:   Those children, when they grow up, do not send their children to church. Only they have a historical understanding of the faith.

Generation 4:   The next generation have no contact with the church apart from occasional baptisms, weddings and funerals. None have any knowledge of the faith.[3]

The church has responded to all this with phenomenal creativity. The mushrooming of courses such as *Alpha, Emmaus, Saints Alive, Christianity Explored* and *Start!* has been an enormous blessing. These courses have been specifically aimed at all John Finney's 'generations', who approach the material in different ways, but all the courses have one goal – to help seekers to come to faith in Christ and find a home in a local Christian community which is seeking to work out how to live this new faith in the world today.

What is even more important is how these courses are run. One implication of the discipleship value of *Mission-shaped Church* is to build the confidence of existing church members in the 'gifting and vocation of leaders'. The best courses are lay led. It is often the pattern that a minister

The place of nurture

will lead the first one or two while training up apprentice leaders. Thus in many churches there is a growing body of lay leaders who are released into their potential as leaders. Their faith has frequently grown from their own experience of God in a group and is then passed on organically to others.

When a church shapes itself around a discipleship value the fruit can be astonishing:

- 2 million people have attended courses

- 1 in 6 of those attending courses have become Christians

- Therefore, over one third of a million people have become Christians.[4]

So nurture courses work and are one of the great success stories of the recent history of the Church in this country, which leads me on to the travesty and scandal – the two-thirds of churches that are failing to seize this opportunity for whatever reason.

It is self-evident that most churches find evangelism and mission hard. Through fear, misunderstanding, denial and insecurity, through being faced with change, or through lack of confidence – or a selection of any and all of these – evangelism is a reluctant guest on the agenda of many churches. Yet in our nurture courses we have something which really works!

For all the joy of the many who have found faith through their local church, the bewildering, unanswered question that faces Jane in the story at the start of this section and many others who have found no programme for nurturing both believer and non-believer: 'If they think this news is so good, why won't they tell me about it?'

More positively, the question each church needs to ask is: 'Where is our church's spiritual growbag? Where is the place for new life?' It's a question to which in God's providence there are many possible answers today.

Small groups as tools for transformation

Nurture courses are also successful because they are about the renewal of the Church. Sadly, many churches that do run nurture groups stop after the first few times. The process usually runs like this:

1st course:	Mainly churchgoers, numbers are good and a lot of enthusiasm is generated.
2nd course:	Fewer churchgoers, one or two from the fringe of the church, numbers are fewer and there is less excitement.
3rd course:	Still fewer churchgoers (usually the more reticent), one or two from outside the church, a couple come to faith/confirmation, but numbers are fairly low.

At this point, many churches stop. The novelty has worn off, fear of failure and of simply not having enough people means that the whole thing is consigned to that ever-expanding drawer labelled 'We tried that for a while but it doesn't work'.

And yet it is at this point that churches that stick the course really begin to see fruit. From this point on, having a place for nurture becomes an intentionally evangelistic, invitational exercise.

story story story story At St John's Church, Burscough, the church runs two basics courses each year, and has done so for the past ten years. Neil Short the vicar explains his approach: 'At the back of my diary is a page of people I have invited and am continuing to invite – families of the bereaved, contacts from school, husbands of existing church attendees, people I meet in the community. When I meet them I invite them. When I see them again, I invite them again, and when the course has finished, there is always something else for them to come onto, such as another course, a parish weekend or into the main family of the church. I am always seeking out and inviting new people.'

A poorly conceived nurture programme assumes that after however many weeks the course runs for, those on the course are fully ready to be part of the church family. It tries to force people out of the incubator too soon and leaves some struggling to survive. Nurture should not be seen as something the Church does for a while; it should take its place within the full picture of discipleship as a whole-life process, expressed relationally and with a desire to transform both the individual and the world.

Just as the Church can waste its time by driving a wedge between evangelism and the struggle for justice in God's world, so also there is a false distinction to be made between the transformational mission value and the discipleship value. The fact is that they flow from one another, our awareness of God's transforming love leading us to share that transforming love.

So churches in their small local discipleship groups should be asking the question, 'How can this faith make a difference not just to us, but to the community in which we live?' Some groups have begun prayer networks and chains; others have been the driving force behind such initiatives as Posada.[5] Others again have been more directly practical in working out their discipleship in the public arena.

> story
> story
> story
> story
> At St John's Church, Werrington, near Peterborough, the church house groups were each given £100 from the church to use to 'bless the community'. Each group used the money for a variety of purposes – to tidy local gardens, clean cars, plant flowers in a neglected public place, offer free food.

Worship and discipleship: one life

In Chapter 3, on worship, I tried to focus on the meaning of liturgy. It is the work of God and of the people of God. In this spirit, many nurture/home/ fellowship groups are developing their expressions of worship through allowing each member of the group to take a lead in worship. In some situations this expression may be very different from what the church provides on a Sunday. For some a more quiet reflective approach will help them in their nurture, for others a more free and informal style will be appropriate. In some nurture groups, permission needs to be given to develop patterns of prayer and to express this often new or renewed relationship with God. Operating in a mission-shaped way means not assuming that Sunday will take care of worship, but integrating it more into this and every aspect of the church's life.

Discipleship and spiritual direction

In 2005 and 2006 the television series *The Monastery* and *The Convent* both showed powerfully the importance of hospitality, time, care and just plain being there in nurturing a faith. In these programmes millions of people watched a small number of men and women spending time with religious communities, experiencing a life of prayer and being challenged head-on in their own spiritual journeys. The religious communities have always been safe places, sanctuary for those journeys to develop powerfully and gently. They have become places of life for those who have been willing to open up. Key disclosure moments have come when individuals or small groups have been able to open up in such a way as to reveal the light of Christ. This could only take place because of the quality of relationships. This has implications for the local church. In the parish community the nurture groups can provide the same sort of safe place to meet with others and with God. It is the presence of Jesus incarnate in the lives of those within such a group which has such a powerful part to play in shaping a church for mission.

Try for a moment to imagine what it would be like to be an expectant mother who has gone into labour, and arrives at the local hospital only to find the hospital staff saying 'We don't do babies here.' If I was about to have a baby, I know where I would go – I would seek out a hospital with a maternity ward. If I was a farmer and wanted new chicks to have the best start in life, I would find a safe environment with the warmth and incubation they needed to live and prosper.

A church which is shaped by mission will bear all the values of mission and will find them most clearly in small communities meeting in people's homes. It may not be called a 'nurture group' – indeed, let's be honest, it's not the greatest name – but whatever it's called, it will be a place of maturing into the fullness of new life in Christ. Let's keep this phenomenon growing!

9

We can't go on meeting like this: shaping the structure of the local church for mission

Tim Sledge

> Seeing a gang of ram-raiders in action, a courageous vicar
> parked his car in such a way as to block the gang's vehicle.
> He then locked the doors and waited for the police. The gang
> threatened him and battered his car but he sat tight. At the
> subsequent trial the judge commended his courage. He
> responded, 'Your honour, for twenty years I've been chairing
> church meetings. Organized crime holds no terrors for me.'

If the mission of God is holistic, then none of the realities of local life should
be outside it. And yet in the midst of all the fine talk about mission and
vision in the local parish church sit the legal and relational realities of making
an organization work. How can these things also be more open to the
values of mission? In this chapter I explore that question and offer some
practical suggestions.

Parochial Church Council meetings

Have a look at these. Is the first or the second more typical of a PCC
meeting in your experience?

> I love going to PCCs! In fact, when the agenda comes, I am
> excited and looking forward to how we are going to discuss
> and work with God's big plans for our small church. We get
> on well, we have fun – in fact they are a really important time
> of fellowship for me, because we pray together and study the
> Bible each meeting and it helps us. We have made some key
> decisions recently, which we have communicated to the rest
> of the church and most people – after all, you can't please
> everyone – are happy and encouraged. But then again, we

only want to discern what is God's way forward for our church!

I have never liked PCC meetings. I have been on the PCC for 30 years since coming to this church. I came here because I fell out with my previous parish priest and wanted to see things done right here. But they are not. We are always having rows – in fact I can't remember a meeting without an undercurrent or without someone getting at someone else. We make all sorts of decisions that no one ever does anything about. Then after the meeting a few of us go to the pub for a drink and say what we didn't say in the meeting and decide to do things differently. I don't know why we don't just cut out the meeting and go to the pub direct!

The simple truth is that the PCC meeting is not usually regarded as the most fruitful aspect of the life of the church – even if it is deemed one of the most important. The pain and grief of St Mungo's in Chapter 1 is duplicated across the country – maybe even in your own local situation. So how can PCCs be engines for mission and how can they be shaped around values which make them models of good practice? In other words, can the machinery of the church facilitate the mission of the church?

In this chapter I'll look at the historical functions of the PCC and ask whether we have lost our way and need to reclaim vision for church governance and management. I am very well aware that the ground being covered may appear all too familiar and thoughts of offering grannies evening classes on 'mission-shaped egg sucking' may come to mind! But we want to help leaders and PCC members to reflect afresh on current working practices and see if and where these can be developed and improved for the sake of the gospel and the life of the local church. The truth that many PCCs may need to face is that, as the title of this chapter implies, we have to stop meeting as we are and find a new way of meeting in both spirit and substance in order that the work of the PCC may bear fruit for the sake of the gospel.

What's the point of the PCC?

> At a recent gathering of PCC members over one week in
> one particular diocese in the Church in Wales (where the
> statutes are almost identical to the Church of England), over
> 500 PCC members were asked what the general functions of
> a PCC were. Of those present over a number of evenings,
> only two people knew or were willing to offer the
> information.

This group was probed further as to the point of the PCC and to explain
its functions. The vast majority had never thought about the question, let
alone formulated an answer. For many church members, the PCC happens
because it has always happened and its purpose is whatever is on the
agenda papers in front of them or whatever is on the more hidden agendas
that members may have brought with them.

By contrast, a clear mission vision is set out in the Parochial Church Council
(Powers) Measure 1956, section 2:

> The PCC and parish priest consult together on matters of
> general concern and importance to the parish.
>
> The PCC's functions include:
>
> • controlling expenditure within the parish
>
> • looking after the maintenance of the building
>
> • co-operation with the minister in promoting in the parish the
>   whole mission of the Church, pastoral, evangelistic, social and
>   ecumenical
>
> • discussing matters concerning the Church of England or any
>   matter of public or religious interest
>
> • having representatives on the deanery Synod.
>
> The PCC should meet at least four times each year.[1]

Of the five functions above, one is evidently in a different league from the rest: 'co-operation with the minister in promoting in the parish the whole mission of the Church, pastoral, evangelistic, social and ecumenical'.

The other four functions, while vital, are clearly designed to support this overarching aim. The local Church Council has a first order role.

If this is so, then on the crowded agenda of any PCC the mission agenda should always sing out the loudest. Is there a way of conducting meetings that fulfils the whole of the 'job specification' of the PCC and enables it to be faithful to the Canons of the Church? How can a PCC reach apostolic boiling point – to use a phrase of Bishop Michael Marshall – and then see everything it does in the light of the mission of God?

For me the answer lies in balancing agendas around the original responsibilities of the PCC. They contain a mission-shaped job description for church members.

Consulting together and with God

First, it shall be the duty of the minister and the PCC to 'consult together on matters of general concern and importance to the parish'.

The PCC is a council, not a board or an executive. It is not a gathering to put heads together and work out what is best for the future of the church. It can be a meeting where heads, hearts and minds are gathered, and people seek the heart of God for his church, and not theirs. Being a member of such a body is an extraordinary honour. In the long history of our local churches, present PCC members and church leaders are entrusted with the care of the church as co-workers with God, consulting together, building on the past history of the people of God in that place, but also seeking God's will in building the future growth and development of the life of the church.

Therefore 'consulting together' must first mean *consulting together with God*.

Most PCC meetings open and close with prayer but these occasions can sometimes feel like a respectful doffing of caps to God, as recognition is given that he might at least be somewhere in the vicinity. Then the meeting progresses as we had always wanted it to! Finally, at the end of the meeting, everything we've discussed is offered to God, who is all of a sudden brought back into the process and given a few moments to catch up with our bright ideas and exciting plans for fundraising and keeping the local street kids out of the building.

Of course this is a parody, but like many parodies, in my experience it contains a good deal of painful truth.

In this book we talk a lot about holistic mission. In doing so we are aware of two things. First, that no Christian would deny that life is indivisible and God is Lord over it all. Secondly, that many Christians are engaged in, and often defeated by, the daily struggle of relating faith to their working lives. That same tension carries over into our church meetings. When faced with a long evening ahead, a thick clump of papers with complex and depressing financial reports, architects' and surveyors' reports, it is all too easy to lose any sense of where God is in all of this. The urgent can crowd out the important – and whenever that happens, the spiritual leaders of the local church need to lay hold on the reality of God through the worship of God.

story
story
story
story

At St Mary's, Luddenden, near Halifax, each PCC was run in the context of the Eucharist. The meeting began at 7.30 p.m. with a Eucharist including a short homily on the Gospel reading. After everyone had received communion, the candles remained lit and the Scriptures open and then the meeting was conducted as per the agenda. At the end of the meeting, the post communion prayer was said and God's blessing pronounced on meeting, discussions and people. Although 30 minutes was taken out of each meeting for worship, most of the business part of the meetings was concluded within 90 minutes.

The impact of this was that a disparate group of people were united not around the agenda, but around communion with God. There were still disagreements, but as fellow sharers in God, there was a greater sense of openness and honesty in addressing and dealing with the matters in hand. They had one eye fixed on the agenda and one eye fixed on God.

Ours is a diverse church, thank God. Every PCC or church group will find a different way of praying. For some, using a more formal office works well, for others a Bible study and reflection, for others some silent prayer, for others perhaps a Eucharist as described above. The style of our prayer and worship is secondary to its importance and centrality in our meetings.

If a difficult decision is to be made or an impasse in discussions has been reached, time should be taken out to stop and pray before moving on. This might happen over the appointment of a parish worker, or a big financial investment such as an organ renovation. This approach is not based on the naive assumption that 'writing will appear on the wall', but a refocused contemplation can provide an anchor point and a check on passions and strongly held opinions. Following the first mission value, it can also remind a group of harassed human beings that God is God.

> For those whose minds are so inclined, planning, analysis and strategizing can be great fun – even addictively so. The risk with moving too quickly with this is that we come to think of God as a poor old soul who cannot really get his act together unless we give him a little training.[2]

Corporate bodies and Christ's body

Legally, the PCC is *a body corporate*[3] - distinct from the people who serve on it, so that no one on the PCC can be made liable for its debts, for example. But perhaps in the light of this legal phrase a PCC might ask itself: Are we truly a body? Are we truly corporate? Does our meeting truly reflect the dignity of the body of Christ as Paul describes it in 1 Corinthians 12?

If this idea sinks into a PCC's corporate awareness, then from a consultation that focuses on God flows an enhanced sense of co-operation with one another. Robert Warren's 'Growing Healthy Churches'[4] process recognizes that a healthy church operates as a community of friendship rather than as a club or religious organization. Relationships are to be nurtured, often in small groups, so that people feel accepted and are helped to grow in faith and service. A healthy church also makes room for all, being inclusive rather than exclusive. If this is true for the church, then how much more should it be the DNA of its leadership. The PCC should be not just a representative microcosm of the church, but should take the lead in modelling Christian community. This has spiritual implications for the PCC members themselves.

Most church councillors represent a particular part of the church community. Annual elections should encourage the widest representation and should emphasize the spiritual and leadership opportunities and responsibilities involved. Many people don't stand for PCC election because the significant time commitment and responsibility seem literally to be more trouble than they are worth. So churches need to look at the frequency and effectiveness of their meetings in the light of their primary purposes.

Alongside purpose, process is also important. Those responsible for the effective running of the PCC can intentionally explore ways to enhance the quality of relationships within the meeting. Often something as simple as 15 minutes spent over refreshments at the start, middle or end of the meeting can help foster a greater sense of belonging. It may be that PCC members undertake to pray specifically for two or three of their peers on the council. One way of doing this is to invite people at the first meeting of the year to commit to praying regularly, building relationships with two people on the church council – one person you relate to naturally, and one person you struggle with. It's good to remind the PCC when introducing this exercise that while you might be thinking of one person you struggle with, they could well be privately thinking of you at the same time!

A hidden agenda?

> We *always* discuss the Summer Fayre at our January meeting.

If our agendas are built on the primary role and responsibilities of the PCC, the statement above may not be so self-evident.

Perhaps at every meeting the PCC might revisit its primary function, highlighted earlier (p. 107):

> Co-operation with the minister in promoting in the parish the whole mission of the Church, pastoral, evangelistic, social and ecumenical.

It's impossible to exaggerate the spiritual dignity that this phrase bestows on a church council. This one sentence, written in ecclesiastical law in 1956, contains all the values of *Mission-shaped Church*.

'Promoting in the *parish*' – a word that comes of course from the Greek word *paroikos*. Rich in meaning, it relates to both geography and mutual accountability, and encompasses both the local church community and the wider part of God's kingdom. Fully understood, it reminds us that when we meet as a PCC we are not a small local club with a limited amount of business to get through; rather, it is our mission to represent God's wider plan to make present his kingdom in our own locality. The *Mission-shaped Church* report echoes this vision: 'A missionary church seeks to shape itself in relation to the culture in which it is located or to which it is called.'[5] I would also want to stress that the term 'parish' explicitly recognizes that the church is not the only agency that will bring about the kingdom of God. Living out the full meaning of the word 'parish' means in turn recognizing other partners, agencies and individuals with whom we can work and 'do kingdom business'.

The 1956 PCC Measure outlines four components of the mission of the church: pastoral, evangelistic, social and ecumenical. Any parish faces a challenge when attempting to get the balance right between the four, and a PCC could spend its time profitably taking part in the following deceptively simple exercise. Imagine you have four baskets and twelve eggs. Each basket represents the pastoral, evangelistic, social and ecumenical components of the PCC agenda. Based on the time you spend on each of these, how many eggs do you put in the different baskets? For example, are all the eggs in the *pastoral* basket or the *ecumenical* one, or are they genuinely evenly spread, and so on? This is a helpful exercise for a church council to do either when reflecting back over a year or when planning ahead to balance its work in all these areas. The exercise could then be repeated, only this time putting eggs in the baskets which the church should be emphasizing over the coming year.

Here are some brief reflections on each of these four areas.

Pastoral In too many churches this is perceived as the domain of the clergy or authorized lay ministers. But the *PCC* is responsible and accountable for the pastoral work of the church. Pastoral work is to do with relationships between one another and ensuring that people are pastored, shepherded.

Evangelistic

> Far from feeling any strong desire or motivation in these
> areas, many PCC members will no doubt feel embarrassed,
> unsuited for that kind of thing or even afraid. You might even
> wish that this section had not been written, but whatever your
> feelings, please read on to the end.[6]

This quotation defining the place of mission from a popular handbook for
PCC members is an honest recognition of the fear and apprehension of
discussing this issue. The PCC is responsible for the local church's emphasis
on how we tell people the good news of Jesus Christ and invite them to
accept him and find a home in the family of God. Many PCCs still seem to
be under the misapprehension that evangelistic work is about large rallies
with charismatic, powerful and vaguely American preachers.

Discussing this area openly and honestly still meets with diffidence and lack
of confidence. In the light of a good deal of bad press, much of it generated
by Christian leaders and pundits, the word 'evangelism' needs both
redeeming and demystifying. Every human being has good news to share
and the basic human instinct when we hear something good is to tell
someone else to share the joy – from the news of a grandchild, to a
surprise encounter, to the state of tomatoes in the greenhouse – whatever
it is, we should be encouraged to share good news. Again, the corporate
culture of a PCC meeting can begin to change with some simple, intentional
sharing of a good news story as part of the meeting or part of the worship.

Social The social role of the PCC is not about arranging socials in the
parish. It is a reminder that church councils have a responsibility not just to
buildings and sustaining churches but to seek to build God's kingdom in the
widest sense. It is not that the local church morphs into the local social
services, but rather that a PCC seeks to promote human flourishing
wherever it can, as part of the mission of God. In this spirit many PCCs
have recently taken the lead on issues such as Make Poverty History, Fair
Trade and ethical shopping, and asylum seekers.

Ecumenical Increasingly, mission opportunities are developing ecumenically as we recognize that we are 'better together'. In our contemporary cultural context, denominational differences are a growing mystery to those outside the Church. For many outside the family of God, we are simply Christians and should work and behave with a sense of shared common purpose.

It is imperative that we begin to reshape our agendas in the light of these big-picture goals. It is not necessary to test people on *Mission-shaped Church* or to demand that people memorize the five missionary values, but simply to ask that each church council the length and breadth of the country revisit the PCC (Powers) Measure of 1956. Annual quiet days and away days for PCC members are invaluable for this sort of refocusing and really set the tone for the year's business. To help with this, many PCCs have used the Growing Healthy Churches material developed by Robert Warren to help them focus and formulate a vision and action plan for the year ahead.[7]

It may also be that a glance at the agendas of our meetings shows that they are already full and there is not time to add in these things – in which case the balance of the agendas needs challenging and redressing. This re-gearing will then produce its own momentum. Because many agendas are shaped by the Matters Arising from the previous minutes, the more the previous minutes are peppered with the whole mission of the Church, the more will be the ensuing meetings!

Meetings, meetings

> We have been saying so many things
> for so many years, without much changing
> and we wonder whether we should stand
> in silence, on this, your holy ground
> and stop our speaking, and our writing
> and our meetings.[8]

The law says that the PCC only needs to meet four times each year. It may decide to meet on other occasions, but it is not, by rights, a monthly event – which it has become in so many churches. Indeed, I think that the whole Church can learn here from the challenges that face rural and multi-parish benefices.

An increasingly common scenario is for a new incumbent to find him or herself responsible for, say, nine parishes – the result of an amalgamation of two benefices. Historically, the individual PCCs have always met bi-monthly. If this continues it would mean that the leader of the parish would be spending 54 evenings each year at PCC meetings – together with the servicing and preparation for these meetings. This represents a huge chunk of time and I would question whether this is time well spent.

Good procedural practice can release energy for mission. Most of the smaller decisions can and should be devolved to the Standing Committee. This is also a useful body to discuss in more detail and see through some matters relating to the fabric of the church, and a place to do some detailed thinking and so free up some space for vision and mission on the agenda of the PCC itself. And to get really radical, the world will not come to an end if the treasurer fails to give a report on the finances of the church at every PCC meeting.

If decision making is done well then there is no need for too many meetings, but an increased need for regular communication in between those meetings.

Team ministries often find themselves with even more meetings than others. One of the many important findings of Bob Jackson in *The Road to Growth*[9] is that team ministries have suffered from a greater decline than the average benefice. One of the possible reasons for this is that setting up teams and looking after teams can generate so many meetings discussing structure and plans and rotas that the actual mission of the Church gets lost. This salutary tale from Russia illustrates the point:

> In 1918, the leaders of the Russian Orthodox Church met in Russia in a remote wooded retreat for a number of weeks. They were incommunicado as they discussed weighty matters of church state and prayed together. One of the key areas of dispute and debate was which colour of vestments to wear on particular feast days. After a few weeks they reappeared back into reality from their meetings only to discover that the Russian revolution had happened, that the church was

nowhere to be seen or found and from being at the heart of the monarchy, they were now marginalized and facing an underground existence for the best part of a century. But at least they had agreed on the colours of the vestments . . . It was a shame they had nowhere to wear them!

So team ministries and multi-parish benefices need to look even more closely at the number of meetings and see whether there is any duplication which could stop in order to 'keep the main thing the main thing'.[10]

 During 2006, the Solihull Team Ministry worked together on a 'Going for Growth' programme. The staff team and others spent time together 'keeping the main thing the main thing'. Care was taken in developing a programme to ensure that all DCCs were on board and working together, with both preparatory meetings and a day away to work on a vision and a strategy for the vision to both change the mindset of the church and also to develop a programme across the team to deliver on the vision. Each church and DCC prioritized this and made space in all their agendas to discuss it. They are united as a team in both leadership and council membership around the one common goal to 'go for growth', but each church is expressing that in its own appropriate and distinctive way.

Decision making

 In 2001, a new incumbent looked at the PCC agenda just handed to her for the first meeting. She then read back through previous minutes and agendas of the past few years to find that an issue over the position of some pews appeared as a regular occurrence in the minutes – often with the words 'No further action to report' against the item. Further investigations led her to discover that for over seven years the matter of some unwanted pews had been discussed at least twice a year. Not only had nothing been done about these pews, but clearly there was no evidence of being able to make a decision.

Clearly, the PCC in the story above had failed to understand the meaning of the word 'agenda' – which means 'the things to be *done*'!

A new Christian was invited to join the local PCC because of his skills in business and decision making. After three meetings he resigned from the PCC – citing the inability to make decisions for the furtherance of the gospel as his main reason.

Part of the work of Springboard, the Archbishops' initiative for the Decade of Evangelism, was to offer PCCs a model to help them make decisions and make them better, and to see through the consequences of decisions made and actions taken.

They produced the model above – designed to help PCCs to work methodically but also to work reflectively and generously in a way which is clear and honouring to all. It works!

- For example, a church wants to develop its children's work with the desire to attract more children to its worship.

- A number of options are then presented, ranging from retraining Sunday school teachers to developing mid-week worship services after school.

- Those options are then discussed openly considering the pros and cons of each one and evaluating the implications for the wider church.

- After some time of reflection and prayer, the decision is made to start a new service in the school after about 18 months of planning and working with the local schools and training up leaders.

- This is all part of the implementation of the plan, which is monitored by a small group of the PCC and outside help from others with expertise in this area.

- The PCC then agrees to discuss the progress each year and to respond to the progress of the project.

This is one way to respond to an issue effectively so as to allow the machinery of church governance to be a sluice-gate to the mission of God, rather than a dam.

To chair or not to chair?

Personally, I was never either taught or trained to chair a PCC or meeting. I found it hard to concentrate on moving an agenda on, discern what was going on in the room, manage the discussions and referee two people who saw opposite sides on almost every issue! In many instances, it can be useful if the vice-chairman actually chairs the meetings even when the parish priest is present. In other instances, the chairing of meetings can alternate between chairman and vice-chairman – and this often has the added edge of competition as each vies for the shortest or best-run meeting!

The Annual Parochial Church Meeting

Each year in America, the President delivers the 'State of the Union' address. It is usually an up-beat assessment of the American nation, reflecting on the past year and providing hope and a vision for governance of the country in the year ahead. It also marks a line in the sand or reference point for the American people as they look forward to the challenges and opportunities of the coming year. The annual budget statement by the Chancellor of the Exchequer in Britain performs a similar function.

Likewise, the annual meeting is a wonderful opportunity for the local church to lay out its plans and discern God's vision for the year ahead. Sadly, too much of the time is taken up with the minutiae of elections, appointments and receiving reports.

But the annual meeting is also the place for the parish's leaders to set out their understanding of God's vision for the future – a 'State of the Kingdom' type address. This may have been worked out at a PCC or Parish Away Day in the run-up to the meeting. A church that has a sense of hope because it knows where it is going is a church that mirrors Christ in his clarity and resolute faithfulness to his own calling.

Shaping the annual meeting around a mission agenda means seeking God's vision for the future, building the community of faith around a common cause to continue to grow the kingdom of God in your own locality. Because the meeting of the new PCC happens very soon after this annual meeting, the agenda of the PCC can begin to be shaped around this key vision statement. If the church is in interregnum, then there is no reason why the churchwarden cannot do the same – or indeed a rural dean or archdeacon.

The deanery synod

> A group of Anglicans waiting to go home.
> (A deanery synod as defined by a retired archdeacon)

> Deaneries have the potential to bring together a range of human and financial resources, to consider mission across parish boundaries, and to share prayer and encouragement.

> Each diocese should consider whether its deanery arrange-
> ments are best organized and employed to encourage the
> mission of the Church, particularly among people in cultures
> and networks not currently connected with church.
>
> (*Mission-shaped Church*, recommendation 5)

The deanery synod might not at first be thought of as a tool for mission –
or indeed imbued with the values which can facilitate a church shaped by
mission – but it could be! Synods could live up to the meaning of their name
– from two Greek words which mean 'the way' and 'together'.

Before addressing the workings of the synod, it is worth affirming or
reaffirming the importance of deaneries. One of the key findings of the
Mission-shaped Church report is that local indigenous expressions of the
gospel are where God is clearly at work. There are numerous examples of
local expressions bubbling up across parish boundaries yet within the
influence of a deanery – and these need the support of the local churches
as they move 'on the way together'.

story
story
story
story

In the Diocese of Peterborough, each deanery is
being asked to develop its own mission plan,
which includes suggestions for deployment of
clergy and the payment of the parish share. The aim is to see
where shared human resources might be made available and
released into supporting the growth of the Church. In the
climate of the 'mixed-economy Church', deaneries are also
being asked to make bids for monies and staffing from a
Diocesan Mission Fund to encourage new ways of being the
Church in designated and agreed areas.

This is one example of the way a number of dioceses are seeking to address
mission and evangelism structurally, while allowing local people to make
decisions locally and support, rather than envy and denigrate, what might be
going on in a neighbouring parish.

There is much more that could be expanded on here, but the same
principles and values of operating as a church council apply to deanery

synods in many of the same ways. Wouldn't it be good if your deanery synod was considered as 'the place to be' to discuss big plans of collaborating together in developing new mission opportunities! And if it would be good, then you can make it so.

Conclusion

Our structures often get a bad press and are treated cynically and given a hard time within the Church itself. But many of the local structures of the Church are indeed shaped very well for mission. Sadly, in many cases, they have gone from being mission-shaped to being manipulated. They have become talking shops rather than places of sharing, discipleship and action for the sake of the kingdom in the community they are serving.

The Church's councils can act as a microcosm of the Church as it should be. They can adopt a lifestyle which is open, honest and rooted in God and committed to seeking the advancement of the kingdom. If they do, then the structures of the Church can and do work well for mission. In many cases, they simply need revisiting, challenging and putting back on the tracks from which they have become derailed – invested with mission values, set firmly on a mission agenda from our loving and sending God.

10 Mission-shaped cathedrals
Mark Rylands

A fresh doorway?

Much of my work in local churches involves trying to engender a strong sense of community among the congregation, enthusing and imparting an understanding of God's mission and care for the wider community and encouraging an overall outward focus of the church. While many churches are growing numerically, more are declining in numbers and becoming more elderly in constitution. In the cathedral where I serve there has been little emphasis on nurturing a sense of belonging through small groups and not much outward focus on mission. The congregations of cathedrals in England (though largely elderly in constitution) are, however, growing numerically,[1] and cathedrals have been heralded as 'the success story of the Church of England in the late twentieth century'.[2]

Superficially, in the light of this report and of current missional thinking, the cathedral is an enigma. It seems to pay little attention to its cultural context, appears to be shaped more by its worship and building than its mission, and yet thrives on a traditional 'come to us' approach. Why?

Is it because cathedrals offer an easy entry point for spiritual searchers without the anxiety of being cajoled into belonging to the Christian community before they are ready? Maybe cathedrals have the potential to be a fresh expression of church, or at least a fresh doorway, for a generation who feel disconnected with the church organization and are more content 'to believe without belonging'.

Education and spirituality

At Chester Cathedral, the education officer Judy Davies runs a week of 'Pilgrim Days' every year. Aimed specifically at Year 5 pupils, Judy defines pilgrimage as a personal journey to a specific place. She outlines the historic purpose of pilgrimage as visiting a special place to enhance one's standing with God, understand something more clearly, pray for a particular concern, obtain forgiveness, do a penance, and experience a sense of personal fulfilment. Her aim is not only to educate the children with historical facts but to give them space to think, enjoy themselves and experience the cathedral as a 'living building'. During the day, the children engage in a variety of activities. Although Judy says she does not evangelize, there is no doubt that during these days the children are encouraged to engage with spiritual matters, not just historical facts. The pilgrimage days are not aimed at church schools – the majority of children are not from a Christian background. She says, however, that many children bring their parents back to visit the cathedral, such is the impact on them.

At Exeter Cathedral a 20-minute interactive pilgrimage service has been designed to involve the children – body, mind and soul. After some workshop activities the children gather, as pilgrims, outside the cathedral; they are met by a member of the clergy and a verger, and incense is wafted over them. (We tell them this is because they are a holy people, cherished by God – and in case any of them, like their medieval counterparts, are a bit smelly!) They enter the cathedral and stop at the font to be sprinkled with water, reminding them of God's welcome and new life for them. They then process up the nave to the crossing to stop at the crucifixion triptych, where the children are encouraged to look at the vivid painting and ask questions. The story of Jesus' crucifixion and resurrection is told. We say 'sorry' prayers and the children are invited to 'kiss' the cross (as pilgrims hundreds of years ago would have done). We then move further eastward up the north aisle to the tomb of Edward Lacy – known for being a saintly man with healing gifts. The children see how the stone on the tomb has been worn smooth from the touch of thousands of pilgrims over the years asking for help and healing. The children are encouraged to name friends or family members who are sick and about whom they are concerned. We sing a simple chant as a prayer and hold a silence together asking for God's healing power and presence with those that have been named. Finally, the children proceed to the very eastern end of the cathedral – the Lady Chapel – where they view the icon of Mary and hear how she offered herself to God and was obedient to him. The children are here invited to light a candle, offer their hopes and make a response to God, if they wish.

There was an initial anxiety on behalf of the instigators of the pilgrimage service that it was verging on proselytizing. However, feedback from teachers who attend (often with little or no faith) has been very positive. They like the fact that the service involves movement and is not sedentary, that it is tactile and engages imagination. They have observed that it stimulates the children's minds and offers them an opportunity to open up to spiritual matters. The teachers also respond warmly to the opportunity for the children to pray for those who are sick or in trouble. Some of the teachers themselves have evidently found the experience personally 'moving' and helpful. It may well be significant that all the teachers present have been under 40 years of age.

Our experiential culture demands more from cathedral education programmes than simply interpreting signs and symbols and giving ten key facts about the cathedral's history. If we do not offer the opportunity of a spiritual experience when children come to the cathedral, we are not only missing an evangelistic window, we are also not adhering to the requirements of the 'secular' National Curriculum or meeting the expectations of the teachers. In today's postmodern culture there is a danger that some cathedrals may not be seen as spiritual enough in their work with children.

Through an experience that explores the history of the building, the life of its community and the gospel story on which it is all founded, the children are invited on a spiritual journey that does not stop at the end of the day's visit. The *Mission-shaped Church* report highlights the 'time-bomb' that is ticking away, as fewer and fewer children are involved in Sunday schools and clubs. Among many other things, the mixed-economy Church means that, along with the emergence of local mid-week clubs in schools, trips to cathedrals are playing a role in keeping the Christian story alive among children in our society.

Pilgrimage and hospitality

story
story
 story
 story

Wakefield Cathedral launched 'Discovery' in February 2005 – a spiritual journey through the building. Discovery is advertised as an audio tour with a difference. It invites visitors to the cathedral to use places and artefacts to reflect on their own unique spiritual journey. Aimed at adults and older teenagers, the experience is enhanced by recordings of the cathedral choir and music staff. In interview, Canon John Holmes revealed that he intended to 'be upfront with visitors about the opportunity to make a spiritual journey' because the research they undertook in 2003–4 revealed what others have found – a society with a growing ignorance of the Christian faith and yet obvious spiritual hunger. Interestingly, the increasing acceptance of spirituality as a desirable aspiration for all people is affirmed here by the fact that Discovery has prompted support from Wakefield City Council and Wakefield Civic Society. They recognize 'its valuable addition to the region's spiritual and cultural heritage'.

story
story
story
story

In Exeter in March 2004, a Saturday prayer day for all ages was organized and advertised through the diocesan news and databases. Hardly anyone from the diocesan church family came. There were 18 at the opening service in the cathedral nave at 10 am and 12 of those were leaders and helpers for the day. There were some calls to 'pack up and go home' but it was decided to persist. Different kinds of prayer stations were set up all around the cathedral – a desert for quiet contemplation in one chapel, praying with bubbles in another. At one station there was a map of the world spread out, with nightlights that could be lit and placed wherever one chose on the map. At another, there was a fishing net suspended over a swathe of blue shiny paper, with an invitation to cut out a fish shape, write on it the name of a person to come to Christ and then place it in the net. At another station there was a small pile of stones before a cross with an invitation to 'build a cairn of hope' by adding a stone, remembering those who carry heavy burdens, and placing them and their needs before the Burden Bearer. At another, there was a 'prayer tree' where coloured ribbons could be tied on to branches with an encouragement to pray for friends, family, colleagues or oneself to grow in faith. In a quiet chapel two people were available with oil to offer anointing with prayer.

The day was intended as a teaching day for the church family to see the potential of prayer stations. What transpired was an effective evangelistic encounter as hundreds of visitors entered the cathedral and engaged with these prayer stations. They just happened to be there – most were tourists, some

> pilgrims, some in distress and actively looking for solace and help. Several were tearfully thankful for being given the opportunity to 'nail their prayers to the cross' or 'receive oil and prayer for healing'. This was a public who generally did not attend church services yet were spiritually open and searching.

One of the key mission values of *Mission-shaped Church* is that a missionary Church is focused on God the Trinity, understanding that mission starts in the heart of God. The Church is called to be a reflection of the divine in its community life, its welcome and its hospitality. Cathedrals are surely right to pay much attention to this aspect of their ministry. For the gospel presents us with a God who in Christ comes running to meet us, embraces us with love, opens the door to let us into his presence and then stands back so that we may have space to be and grow. God's welcome is a homecoming.

Alongside this, pilgrimage too makes increasing sense in a postmodern society. The idea is also widely embraced in the Church because conversion is increasingly being seen as process rather than event. As Mike Booker and Mark Ireland note: 'Peter's journey to faith occupies the whole of the period of Jesus' ministry, and if there is a conversion moment it cannot be definitely identified.'[3]

Cathedrals are well placed to help people on this journey in life and faith. The linking of a place of divine revelation with the dynamic of movement – a journey – which is such a helpful symbol for Christian function and life, seems to be why pilgrimage is evangelistically effective. Through hospitality and pilgrimage, cathedrals can bring the glories of their heritage to bear on the spiritual hunger of people today. Thirteen years ago, Graham Cray observed that

> Postmodern people are more likely to come to faith through experience . . . But one of the tragedies of today is that some elements of the Church are now so firmly secularized in their disbelief of the supernatural that they have nothing to say to a culture which increasingly takes spirituality and the supernatural for granted.[4]

Worship and evangelism

In a denomination that has declined by over 15 per cent in the past 15 years, cathedrals are seen by many as, to repeat Bishop Inge's phrase, 'the success story of the Church of England'.[5] Attendances at regular weekly services in cathedrals have steadily increased by a total of 17 per cent since the turn of the millennium. Nationally, 16,000 adults and 2,500 children and young people are usually present at Sunday services alone, while over the whole week the figures rise to 24,000 and 6,000 respectively.[6] My own investigations at Exeter Cathedral show that average Sunday communicants rose from 251 in 2001 to 292 in 2004.

You would be hard pressed to find a cathedral chapter that did not see the excellence of their worship as the main reason for these growing attendances. *Mission-shaped Church* recognizes the increase in attendance at cathedrals and is aware of new congregations that have grown based on the use of the traditional, *Book of Common Prayer*, services.[7] It attributes the 'success' to 'people looking for mystery, beauty, stability and a sense of God's presence . . . discovered in forms and styles that reflect the Church's heritage in liturgy and spirituality, and a sense of sacred stability in a fast changing world'.[8]

All this 'success' is real enough, but it needs to be put in perspective. Much of this growth is due to the fact that lapsed Christians have found, in the anonymity and special presence of a cathedral, a way back into the faith and the path of discipleship.

Mission-shaped Church brings a challenge here to cathedrals as well as local churches. It is the worship style of a church that is often its key shaping factor – the central characteristic around which people choose to 'shape' themselves together into churches. Churches and cathedrals are not generally shaped by God's mission and certainly not by evangelism. We seem to have ended up with 'worship-shaped churches', churches where the worship style is what gives people their essential sense of belonging.[9] This is even more emphatically so in cathedrals, where people travel great distances to attend worship. The perceived success and numerical growth of cathedral congregations may, therefore, be leading to a complacency about whether they need to be engaged in mission and evangelism. There is a danger that some cathedrals, particularly those with a great musical tradition, may be focusing primarily on being centres of worship (and not also centres of mission) because it is the traditional worship that currently attracts regular Sunday worshippers. If, however, this growth is really transfer growth and not new disciples, then there will be problems in the long term.

Even so, cathedrals seem to engage with pre-Christians better than many other large and growing churches. One reason is that they act like sacred theatres, attracting many people within their walls for all sorts of reasons – beauty, architecture, atmosphere. This temple-like presence and majesty of a cathedral, combined with Scripture, prayers, a few well-chosen words and beautiful music, has the ability to catch people off guard and fill them with a sense of awe. It prompts them to ask the big questions concerning the meaning of life.

Secondly, cathedrals 'act like religious railway stations'[10] where all sorts of people turn up to services with different destinations in mind. Big services offer a safe space and anonymity in that many people are there and no one is expected to talk to their neighbour; not being local is an advantage – unknown, it is possible to be lost in the crowd and to listen and respond without fear of being coerced into a commitment one is not ready to make.

There are also particular advantages for an evangelistic ministry, in that people are not automatically labelled 'Christian' if they go to the cathedral. There is little fear of 'Christian stigma' being attached to them by their peers, and therefore cathedrals can be, for them, laboratories of the spirit – places where it feels safe to experiment and explore spiritual matters.

A particular evangelistic opportunity for cathedrals through their worship would appear to be their civic ceremonies and links with the city and council (see Chapter 7 above). There is much in Scripture to make us cautious of state religion, yet to shun it leads to the danger of producing an unincarnational faith unrelated to the world. Certainly the role of the cathedral must not descend into merely consecrating the status quo. However, total rejection of the civic authorities will lead to the Christian community becoming a ghetto. A balancing act is called for so that the cathedral is close enough to relate well to the authorities yet also distinct enough to challenge them with the claims of the gospel.

On a personal level, cathedrals can offer quiet dialogue and pastoral care of people in political or public office who rarely find an understanding ear or supporting arm elsewhere.[11] Such people are often 'too busy' to be involved or even known in the local community where they live, yet they come into contact with the cathedral through their work duties – attendance at mayoral and legal services, particular civic carol services and concerts, university degree ceremonies and the like. This is where the cathedral gets its label of ministry 'to the great and the good'. Cathedrals do not minister to these alone, but there is certainly an important ministry here. The breadth of this ministry can be seen to spring from Jesus' own ministry to two very different characters – Zacchaeus and Nicodemus. People who have elbowed and cheated their way to positions of power and influence are often people of low self-esteem. The gospel of grace and acceptance can speak powerfully to the Zacchaeuses of this world. Equally, those who thought they had goodness and righteousness sewn up and neatly ordered will have their world views challenged and can start a new spiritual journey, like Nicodemus. Through hearing the gospel at civic ceremonies, combined with hospitality given and friendships made, many of our public servants have come to faith, or come back to faith, through this evangelistic ministry of cathedrals.[12]

Furthermore, cathedrals benefit from economies of scale. If the parish churches of the Church of England used to be seen as 'good boats to fish from' by evangelists, then cathedrals act like huge trawlers where every variety of humanity gets caught up in the nets. Adrian Newman, the Dean of Rochester, is passionate about leading 'a cathedral community that faces outward as a servant to the city and diocese and that has an apostolic role'.[13] He sees that cathedrals can play an important role evangelistically by 'engaging with a range of people whose spirituality, lifestyle and morality is often questionable and unorthodox. We need a positive approach to be adopted to where people are *now* – rather than where we would like them to be.'[14] This sentiment chimes theologically with St Paul, who emphasized how 'while we were yet sinners, Christ died for us' (Romans 5.8).

At Manchester Cathedral, Canon Robin Gamble has undertaken evangelistic events that focus on the cathedral congregation and its wider community. 'A Time for All', in 2002, involved a diversity of organizations and sought to bring them together, closer to each other and closer to God. Bistro meals, an open day with trips up the tower, art and craft displays and bell-ringing demonstrations all gave the feel of a church fête. Interspersed among this activity were short services and a video showing *The Miracle Maker*. On the Sunday, invitation services were held. The weekend was popular and followed up in subsequent years by 'Angels' in 2004 and 'The Lion, the Witch and the Wardrobe' in 2005.

In pursuing this approach, Robin has been adopting the traditional 'Come to Us' evangelistic strategy of the Church which *Mission-shaped Church* predicts will become less effective as we find fewer people on the fringes of the church and more people who are unchurched. Cathedrals with their economy of scale are perhaps able to continue this strategy longer than local churches. A large congregation means there will be a good number of contacts – friends and relations – who can be invited to attend such an event. Robin feels strongly, however, that it is not a matter of either 'go to them' or 'come to us', but of both. The events he put on with the help of the cathedral community attracted many people who were not invited but 'who just happened to be passing by'. Thus Robin's approach aims to build on the 'returner' policy of welcoming back the prodigals as well as reaching out to the unchurched. A 'Back to Church' Sunday scheme organized in Manchester Diocese in 2004 led to 800 new church members, some of whom were at the cathedral.

This 'mixed-economy' approach to evangelism at cathedrals may be more effective than one aimed solely at the open dechurched or at the unchurched. For evangelistic opportunities, therefore, cathedrals would seem to have a unique position among churches. Their central location in a city combined with their high public status means that they encounter many unchurched people. Their large congregations also mean that there is a sizeable church fringe of people who may be responsive to invitations.

Conclusions? No, more questions!

Cathedrals can rightly take their place in the mixed-economy Church. The evangelistic opportunities for cathedrals remain favourable. In their worship setting and service to the wider society they are obviously building bridges, Christ is being revealed and some people are becoming disciples as a result.

The biblical evidence warns of the dangers of focusing narrowly and complacently on God's presence in the Temple. For God's people to forget the outward focus of this mission is to lose sight of the pilgrim God whose care is for the whole creation. His presence is found primarily in human beings – Jesus Christ, his community of followers and unexpected people on the margins. The review of Scripture indicates that cathedrals must remember that they are first and foremost a Christian community, not a building – called to be bearers of the divine presence, an embodiment of the good news and beacons of God's Spirit to a society that walks in darkness.

A 'mission-shaped cathedral' needs good leadership and an outward missionary vision. The greater involvement of bishops in cathedral ministry may well have the effect of directing that focus outward to the needs of the diocese (Michael Sadgrove, the Dean of Durham Cathedral, has for a long time proposed a closer collaboration between bishop and dean in evangelistic activity). At the moment, cathedrals seem to be in a 'magnetic mode' of mission, drawing people into their worshipping community. If they are to play a significant role in the re-evangelization of this country in the future, the findings of the *Mission-shaped Church* report indicate that they will need to rediscover their apostolic shape of former centuries because we now face a society that is becoming rapidly unchurched and pagan.

When a river begins to run dry the fish will collect in the deep pools where there is still some oxygen and food. Eventually, however, if the drought continues, even the deep pools will run dry – it is just that the deep pools feel the effects of drought last of all. The challenge for cathedrals today is to be more than the deep pools that attract the last life of a dying church. Rather, as they build on the values of mission, this chapter aims to show the potential for cathedrals to become deep well-springs that revitalize the

Church and transform a world that is thirsty. It has happened before.
With God's grace, a visionary leadership, and the motivation of the
Christian community, there is no reason why cathedrals cannot take their
place at the heart of the mixed economy and become centres of apostolic
mission again.

Afterword
Tim Sledge

Just to recap, the *Mission-shaped Church* report provides a snapshot of new, different shapes of Christian community that are bubbling up all over the country. But the report also provides a theology of church-based mission and some values for that mission, which are valid for inherited church as so many people live it today. These values contain a deep longing for the kingdom of God to come. To desire and work for a mission-shaped parish is not a nostalgic hankering after the past nor an itchy longing for the future, but a passionate realization of what already is and the potential that still lies in the Church as we have received it.

However we dress it up, we need to make sense of God's mission in a changing world, and that requires all our creativity and vitality. To cite one example of the shift in our context, in 1950, over 50 per cent of children in this country attended Sunday school. By 2003, this figure had reduced to 3 per cent. Bob Jackson notes, in *Hope for the Church*, that 'very few adults without a Sunday school background become worshippers in later life'.[1]

And so, whether we like it or not, the models of our ministry are changing. This is reflected in the new *Common Worship* ordination service:

> Priests are called to be servants and shepherds among the
> people to whom they are sent. With their bishop and fellow
> ministers, they are to proclaim the word of the Lord and to
> watch for the signs of God's new creation. They are to be
> messengers, watchmen and stewards of the Lord; they are to
> teach and to admonish, to feed and provide for his family, to
> search for his children in the wilderness of this world's
> temptations, and to guide them through its confusions, that
> they may be saved through Christ for ever.

Teaching and pastoring remain. But now there is a distinctive third strand, not present 25 years ago when the ASB Ordinal was introduced. Now the challenge and calling is first to find people – 'to search for his children' – and then teach and pastor them. Now people are being called to a different model of ministry. The recent change in the selection criteria for all those offering themselves for the ordained ministry from 2005 includes this new 'Criterion on Mission and Evangelism':

> You should show an awareness of how changes in culture and society have an impact on the life of the Church. You should also show potential as a leader of mission and a commitment to enable others in mission and evangelism.[2]

No wonder many clergy now, including us as authors, often wryly wonder whether any of us would be selected to train today! Meanwhile we must be frank: for many who have faithfully served over the years there is a feeling of dis-ease and vulnerability which makes clergy afraid – some for their jobs, some for the churches they have sought to serve, and for the kingdom and the Church which they love dearly. With all this around us, where do we turn?

Vulnerable ministry

In response to the sense of anxiety that many are experiencing, I want to affirm roundly that for the Church the mission of God is not about success but about obedience to the God of mission. Being mission-shaped is not about being success-shaped or power-shaped. In the end, if it is real at all, being mission-shaped is about being shaped by and around Jesus.

And the Jesus model of mission is a vulnerable model. Jesus sends his ministers/missionaries in pairs 'like lambs among wolves' (Luke 10.3). We know we are vulnerable – but the good news is that we're called to be vulnerable.

Of course, as we straddle the shifting sands and changes in society and the Church, it is sorely tempting to hang on to what we know. It is understandable, it is totally natural, but it will not do. Vulnerability is the Jesus way. For vulnerability forces us to rely not on heritage or precedent or tradition but on the strength of God.[3]

> The gospel cannot be proclaimed by the strong to the weak,
> but only by the weak to the strong.[4]

And one final thing for all of us, clergy and laity, who lead in the parish church. Before we are called to be vulnerable ministers sharing in the mission Christ has given to us, God has another call. God calls us into life. The God of mission is one whose very nature is to give life through a spending, sending love. And we are primarily receivers from God before we are doers for God.

Spending, sending love. The missionary God who calls is the God who calls into life and who can't help giving himself away. In the very nature of God is this self-giving. To be faithful to this God is to desire to share and give of what we have received – to be generous as God has been generous to us. But we cannot give away what we don't have! Therefore our primary calling is to receive rather than to give.

The vocation into life and the journey on which we embark are not about a busy, frantic getting from one place to another, but about making space, stopping and enjoying the gifts given on the way. Living a mission-shaped life means being resourced by relationships, creation, hobbies, relaxation, even idleness – through which we can see afresh the many ways in which God reveals himself in the world.

We know that this is not always achievable. There are many times when life becomes squeezed by circumstances, expectations and pressure. But when local church leaders lose the acumen and the ability to appreciate God's grace, then there is a vacuum. Anxiety and haste will fill it. Please believe us when we say that we've had enough of anxiety and haste.

The last thing we want to do is to end this book with yet another exhortation geeing up the church – 'Get shaping your church around mission.' But that would not be God's way as we have received it. First and last of all, to ourselves and to you, we want to say, 'Live Abundant Life-Shaped Lives!' And we pray that you will.

Notes

Preface
1. Rowan Williams, Presidential Address to the General Synod, July 2003. For the full text see
   http://www.archbishopofcanterbury.org/sermons_speeches/2003/030714.html
2. George Lings, 'Discernment in Mission', *Encounters on the Edge* 30, April 2006, p. 29.
3. See *Mission-shaped Church*, Church House Publishing, 2004, p. 37.
4. Tim Dearborn, quoted in *Mission-shaped Church*, p. 103.

Chapter 1   The value of values
1. Steven Croft, George Lings and Pete Pillinger, *Moving on in a Mission-shaped Church*, Church House Publishing, 2005, p. 8.
2. Cell-church pioneer Bill Beckham (conference speech).
3. John V. Taylor, *Enough is Enough*, SCM Press, 1975, p. 85.
4. David Bosch, *Transforming Mission*, Orbis, 1991, p. 392 (my italics).
5. *Transforming Mission*, p. 390.
6. *Mission-shaped Church*, p. 81.
7. *Mission-shaped Church*, pp. 81–2.
8. For more on all this see Paul Bayes, *Mission-shaped church: values*, Grove Books, 2004.
9. www.freshexpressions.org.uk
10. John M. Hull, *Mission-shaped Church: a theological response*, SCM Press, 2005.
11. For more on social capital and faithful capital see Ann Morisy, *Journeying Out*, Geoffrey Chapman, 2004; Commission on Urban Life and Faith, *Faithful Cities*, Methodist Publishing House and Church House Publishing, 2006.
12. Irenaeus, *Adversus Haeresis*, IV,20,7.
13. *Emergingchurch.info*, Monarch, 2004, p. 39.
14. In *The Road to Growth*, Church House Publishing, 2005, p. 84.

Chapter 2   That was then ...
1. Declaration of Assent: preface. In, for example, *Common Worship*, Church House Publishing, 2000, p. xi.
2. Bede, *Ecclesiastical History*, book IV.
3. Nick Spencer, *Parochial Vision*, Paternoster 2004, especially chapter 1 'The rise and fall of the English Parish'.
4. Sydney Smith, *Letters of Peter Plymley*, p. 596.
5. Howse, *Saints in Politics*, p. 15 (written in 1952).
6. Lady Knutsford, *Life and Letters of Zachary Macaulay*, E. Arnold, 1900, pp. 271–2.

7. Wilbert Shenk, *Henry Venn*, Orbis, 1983, p. 3.
8. Michael Hennell, *John Venn and the Clapham Sect*, Lutterworth Press, 1958, p. 180.
9. Samuel Wesley, 'Account of the Religious Society Begun in Epworth, in the Isle of Axholm Lincolnshire, Feb:1, An: Dom: 1701–2' (quoted from David Lowes Watson, *The Early Methodist Class Meeting*, Discipleship resources, 1985, p. 194).
10. Wesley, 'Journal', 1742.
11. I owe this analysis of the facts of early Methodist class and band life to the doctoral thesis of Tom Albin, Dean of the Upper Room, Nashville USA. http://www.upperroom.org/
12. Tom Albin, 'Finding God in small groups', *Christianity Today*, August 2003.
13. John Wesley, 'Rules for Bands', 1744.
14. From Fr T. E. Jones' article on the website of St Peter's, London Docks, http://www.stpeterslondondocks.org.uk/section/38
15. Jones' article, St Peter's website.
16. See *Mission-shaped Church*, pp. 87, 96, 104 passim.
17. Andrew Saint, in *The Victorian Church*, Manchester University Press, 1995, p. 30.
18. Malcolm Johnson, *Bustling Intermeddler? The Life and Work of Charles James Blomfield*, Gracewing, 2001, p. 120.
19. Bob Jackson, *The Road to Growth*, Church House Publishing, 2005, p. 98.
20. *The Road to Growth*, p. 101.
21. Diocese of Salisbury, 'The Aldhelm Way', 2005.

Chapter 3 Mission-shaped worship

1. The gist of a quote from Ian Hislop.
2. From *Equus* by Peter Schaeffer.
3. Raymond Fung, *The Isaiah Vision*, WCC Publications, 1992, p. 13.
4. *Mission-shaped Church*, p. 81.
5. William Abraham, *The Logic of Evangelism*, Hodder & Stoughton, 1989, p. 162.
6. Lord Carey, from a speech to the Wakefield Diocesan Conference, 1996.
7. *Let my people speak*: www.churchsurvey.co.uk
8. The Methodist Conference's contribution to the Fresh Expressions movement makes much of the Methodist word 'connexion'. Fresh Expressions material has been greatly enriched by this concept (see www.freshexpressions.org.uk).
9. Extract from the Annual Report of 2005 for Family Care charity.
10. Richard Holloway, *Dancing on the Edge*, Fount, 1997, p. 159.
11. Fung, *The Isaiah Vision*, p. 13.
12. Archbishop George Carey.
13. Pablo Picasso, quoted by Bishop John Hind.
14. For an analysis of different networks see Joe Hasler, 'We have networks too . . .', in *Crucible*, 2006.
15. 'Apt liturgy' is a phrase of Ann Morisy. See for example her *Journeying Out*, Continuum, 2005, pp. 156–64.
16. For more information on the place of the open dechurched within the full mission challenge in our generation, visit www.cofe.anglican.org/info/statistics/

17. Robert Warren, *The Healthy Churches' Handbook*, Church House Publishing, 2004. Leading your church into growth; tim.sledge@peterborough-diocese.org.uk

18. From a priest following a diocesan worship training day.

19. Justin Martyr, 1 Apology 67, taken from Gordon Lathrop, *Holy Things, a liturgical theology*, Fortress Press, 1993, pp. 31–2.

20. This is a phrase and concept developed by Canon Robin Gamble and the Leading your Church into Growth team.

21. Warren, *Healthy Churches' Handbook*, pp. 40ff.

22. Huddersfield Contemporary Music Festival, November 1989.

23. David Ford and Daniel Hardy, *Living in Praise: Worshipping and Knowing God*, Darton, Longman & Todd, 2004.

24. Fresh Expressions, *Moving on in a Mission-shaped Church*, Church House Publishing, 2005, p. 4.

25. Dante, *The Divine Comedy*.

Chapter 4   The chores of grace?

1. A phrase first coined by Canon John Young, former Canon Evangelist in the Diocese of York.

2. David Jones, 'A, a, a Domine Deus' in *The Sleeping Lord*, Faber, 1995.

3. For details see the Church of England web site: www.cofe.anglican.org

4. Stuart Murray Williams, *Post-Christendom*, Paternoster Press, 2004, p. 1.

5. Office for National Statistics. For more details visit www.statistics.gov.uk

6. Bob Jackson, *The Road to Growth*, Church House Publishing, 2005, Chapter 8, pp. 96–110.

7. Alan Billings, *Secular Lives, Sacred Hearts*, SPCK, 2004.

8. From a sermon given by Bishop John V. Taylor.

9. For an excellent unpacking of attractional and missional thinking, see Michael Frost and Alan Hirsch, *The Shaping of the Church to Come*, Hendrickson, 2003.

10. For an excellent unpacking of the church as a service provider, see Ann Morisy, *Journeying Out*, Continuum, 2005, pp.186–7.

11. *Mission-shaped Church*, p. 37.

12. *Mission-shaped Church*, p. 37.

13. *Mission-shaped Church*, p.13.

14. Billings, *Secular Lives, Sacred Hearts*, SPCK, 2004.

15. John Finney, *Finding Faith Today*, British and Foreign Bible Society, 1992.

16. This was not a 'pram service'. Prams don't need Jesus – their contents and pushers do! But for more on shaping church for children, see Margaret Withers, *Mission-shaped Children*, Church House Publishing, 2006.

17. Revd Tim Alban Jones in *The Guardian,* Saturday, 7 August 2004.

18. See David Kennedy, *Common Worship 1*, ideas for All Souls.

19. See Yvonne Richmond, Nick Spencer, Rob Frost, Anne Richards, Mark Ireland and Steven Croft, *Evangelism in a Spiritual Age*, Church House Publishing, 2005, p. 83.

Chapter 5   Mission-shaped Isle of Dogs

1. John Austin Baker, *The Faith of a Christian*, Darton, Longman & Todd, 1996, p. 209.

Chapter 6   Friendship, community and mission

1. *Sojourners* magazine, vol. 9.1, January 1980, quoted in *The Franciscan*, vol. 14 no. 3, September 2002.
2. For more details see Robert Warren, *The Healthy Churches' Handbook*, Church House Publishing, 2004, especially ch. 4 (p. 36) and the resources section (p. 152).
3. *Mission-shaped Church*, p. 82.
4. David Ford, *Self and Salvation*, Cambridge University Press, 1999, p. 159. See also, for example, Christian Schwarz, *Natural Church Development*, Churchsmart Resources, pp. 36ff.; Robert Warren, *The Healthy Churches' Handbook*, Church House Publishing, 2004, pp. 36, 48 etc.; Bob Jackson, *Hope for the Church*, Church House Publishing, 2002, pp. 86ff.
5. Kenneth Child, *In His Own Parish*, SPCK, 1970, p. 15.
6. Alan Bennett, 'Take a Pew', from *Beyond the Fringe*, 1961.
7. Monica Furlong, *C of E: the state it's in*, Hodder & Stoughton, 2000, p. 252.
8. Jürgen Moltmann, *The Open Church*, SCM Press, 1978, p. 51.
9. Moltmann, *The Open Church*, p. 61.
10. *The Open Church*, p. 52.
11. *The Open Church*, p. 53.
12. *The Open Church*, p. 62.
13. Carlo Carretto, *I Sought and I Found*, Orbis, 1984, p. 34.
14. *The Healthy Churches' Handbook*, p. 41.

Chapter 7   On being mission-shaped civic church

1. See website at www.scriptureunion.org.uk
2. Michael Sadgrove, 'A hunger to be more serious: the mission of cathedrals today', in *Transmission*, Bible Society, Spring 1998, p. 13.
3. See Richard Askew, *From Strangers to Pilgrims*, Grove Books, 1997.
4. See www.labyrinth.org.uk
5. Quoted from a 'Resonance' publicity leaflet.

Chapter 8   The place of nurture within a mission-shaped church

1. *Mission-shaped Church*, p. 82.
2. A recent statistic of those who had read Dan Brown's *The Da Vinci Code* suggests that 60 per cent of them believed that Jesus and Mary Magdalene were indeed married.
3. From John Finney, *Emerging Evangelism*, Darton, Longman & Todd, 2004, p. 78.
4. Peter Brierley, *Leadership, Vision and Growing Churches*, Christian Research, 2003.
5. Posada is a travelling crib scheme run in many parishes and promoted by the Church Army. For more details see www.churcharmy.org

Chapter 9   We can't go on meeting like this

1. James Behrens, *Practical Church Management*, Gracewing, 2005.
2. Paul Bayes, *Mission-shaped Church*, Grove Books, 2004, p. 14.
3. For more on the legal status of the church and working effectively and legally, please read James Behrens' excellent *Practical Church Management*.
4. For more, see Robert Warren, *The Healthy Churches Handbook*, Church House Publishing, 2004.
5. *Mission-shaped Church*, p. 81.
6. John Pitchford, *An ABC for the PCC*, Mowbray, 1997, p.113.
7. See Robert Warren, *The Healthy Churches' Handbook*, Church House Publishing, 2005.
8. Dorothy McRae-McMahon, *Liturgies for the Journey of Life*, SPCK, 2000, p. 41.
9. Bob Jackson, *The Road to Growth*, Church House Publishing, 2005; see Chapter 3 in particular.
10. Stephen Covey, *The Seven Habits of Highly Effective People*, Free Press, 1990.

Chapter 10   Mission-shaped cathedrals

1. Figures from the Research and Statistics Department, Archbishops' Council, March 2005.
2. Email correspondence with John Inge, Bishop of Huntingdon and former Vice-Dean of Ely Cathedral, 4 October 2005.
3. M. Booker and M. Ireland, *Evangelism – Which Way Now?* Church House Publishing, 2004, p. 5.
4. G. Cray, *From Here to Where? The Culture of the Nineties*, Board of Mission Paper 3, Board of Mission, 1992.
5. J. Inge, see note 2 above.
6. Figures from the Research and Statistics Department, Archbishops' Council, March 2005.
7. *Mission-shaped Church*, p. 73.
8. *Mission-shaped Church*, p. 74.
9. This idea was stimulated by a conversation with David Muir, the Adult Education Adviser for Exeter Diocese.
10. Interview with Robin Gamble, Canon Evangelist at Manchester Cathedral, 26 September 2005.
11. R. Jeffrey, 'Cathedrals and Society' in Iain Mackenzie (ed.), *Cathedrals Now*, Canterbury Press, 1996, p. 105.
12. Confirmed in email correspondence with Stephen Cottrell, 27 September 2005 and Tom Wright 21 September 2005. From my own observations, there are also several members of the congregation at Exeter Cathedral who fall into this category.
13. Email correspondence with Adrian Newman, 4 October 2005.
14. Email correspondence with Adrian Newman, 4 October 2005.

Afterword

1. Bob Jackson, *Hope for the Church*, Church House Publishing, 2002, p. 00.
2. Quoted in *Ministry in the Church of England*, Ministry Division of the Archbishops' Council, 2005.
3. For more see John Holmes, *Vulnerable Evangelism*, Grove Books, 2003.
4. Quoted by Clifford Longley in *The Tablet*, 2 December 1995.

Index